What a clever way to engage little ones in the great adventure of God! Kids will beg for another page of *Let's Go! Bible Adventures* just to find out what surprising vehicle is on the next page and discover deep Bible truths along the way.

> **CHRISTIE THOMAS,** award-winning author of multiple books for Christian kids, including *Fruit Full: 100 Family Experiences for Growing in the Fruit of the Spirit*

Let's Go! Bible Adventures is the perfect Bible storybook for active littles who love all things transportation. From a monster truck to a rocket ship to an ice cream truck to a bulldozer and fire truck, the next generation will see that even though our modes of transportation have changed, God's love is forever. This creative rhyming collection of Old and New Testament stories is bound to be loved by children and their caretakers.

> **TINA CHO,** author of *God's Little Astronomer, God's Little Oceanographer, My Breakfast with Jesus*, and the award-winning *The Ocean Calls*

From the opening page, I absolutely loved *Let's Go! Bible Adventures*! This delightful book will capture the attention of young readers (including my own kids!) through its engaging poems and beautiful artwork. Even better, it faithfully tells the story of the Bible in a way that will have children falling in love with God's Word. This will be a precious addition to my own children's library, but also a resource for every church's kids' ministry. The message of God's never-changing love could not be more timely for children being raised in our ever-changing world.

> **CURT TAYLOR,** senior pastor of Cherry Hills Community Church

If you'd have told me that one day I'd be reading a faithful retelling of Bible stories that included ice cream trucks, rockets, submarines, and helicopters, I would never have believed you. And yet, here it is, in Valerie Ellis's unbelievably innovative *Let's Go! Bible Adventures*. This is creative Bible story retelling at its finest. Simply brilliant.

> **GLENYS NELLIST**, author of *Love Letters from God*, *I Wonder: Exploring God's Grand Story*, and *Good News! God Loves You*!

Let's Go! Bible Adventures is a delightful and engaging children's book that combines the excitement of transportation with timeless Bible stories. I love how Valerie weaves in all elements of transportation like food trucks, helicopters, bulldozers, boats, and even hot-air balloons! This book is perfect for kids who have a passion for all things transportation-related, making it a fantastic tool for capturing their interest and teaching them Bible stories. And each adventure is beautifully illustrated and wonderfully written!

> **VANESSA MYERS**, children's minister, author, and founder of Family Faith Builders

With *Let's Go! Bible Adventures*, Valerie Ellis has invited kids to embark on an exciting ride through the Bible, discovering God's wonders and care in every story. The transportation theme is a brilliant way to engage busy little minds, and the faithful retelling of both familiar and lesser-known stories ensures a rich and inspiring experience. This book beautifully reminds children that God's love never changes.

> **RYAN RUSH**, PhD, senior pastor of Kingsland Baptist Church, founder of Empowered Homes, and author of *Restore the Table*

This book is a creative and interactive experience! Children will be delighted to learn the truths of the Bible while exploring modern transportation. Grandparents, parents, and even older siblings will love reading this book with little ones.

>   **ERICA RENAUD,** speaker, teacher, and author of *Pray with Me: Help Your Children Engage in Authentic and Powerful Prayer*

One of our favorite ways to connect with our kids and grandchildren is by sharing the fun of a good story. *Let's Go! Bible Adventures* puts a colorful, engaging, and creative book in our hands that shares the truths of God and sparks laughter and conversation too. Kids will discover that despite the differences in transportation and technology from Bible times to now, our mighty and wonderful God never changes. What a great resource to introduce our little ones to God's love!

>   **ROB and JOANNA TEIGEN** of Growing Home Together

Adam and Eve with a tractor? Noah on a cruise ship? A food truck for the five thousand? Of course not! But in *Let's Go! Bible Adventures*, Ellis contrasts these modern-day vehicles with Bible-times transportation—and the results are sure to make little ones giggle, all while teaching them the key stories and truths of the Bible. A joyful, bouncing, rhyming delight!

>   **TAMA FORTNER,** ECPA award-winning and bestselling author of more than sixty titles

An engaging, cleverly written first introduction to God's Word that captures the imagination of preschoolers while pointing them closer to God. Children will love learning Bible stories through the lens of transportation using vehicles like ice cream trucks, helicopters, and even life rafts!

> **LAURA SASSI**, author of multiple books for young children including the My Tender Heart series, *Faithful Feet*, *Goodnight, Ark* and more

Preschoolers have such a great fascination with vehicles, and Valerie Ellis has winsomely linked a simple introduction to biblical narratives with modes of transportation that kids will adore! Each chapter, communicated through succinct rhyming language, weaves the story of God's great love for his people and opens the door for deeper parent/child conversations through questions about transport, bonus Bible facts, and imaginative illustrations. I wholeheartedly recommend this book to all parents and ministry leaders with little ones who love trucks, cars, trains, and planes, and pray that through their love of vehicles they fall in love with God's Word!

> **LINDSEY SCHULTZ**, children's ministry director, Redeemer Presbyterian Church, East Side, New York City

Let's Go!
Bible Adventures

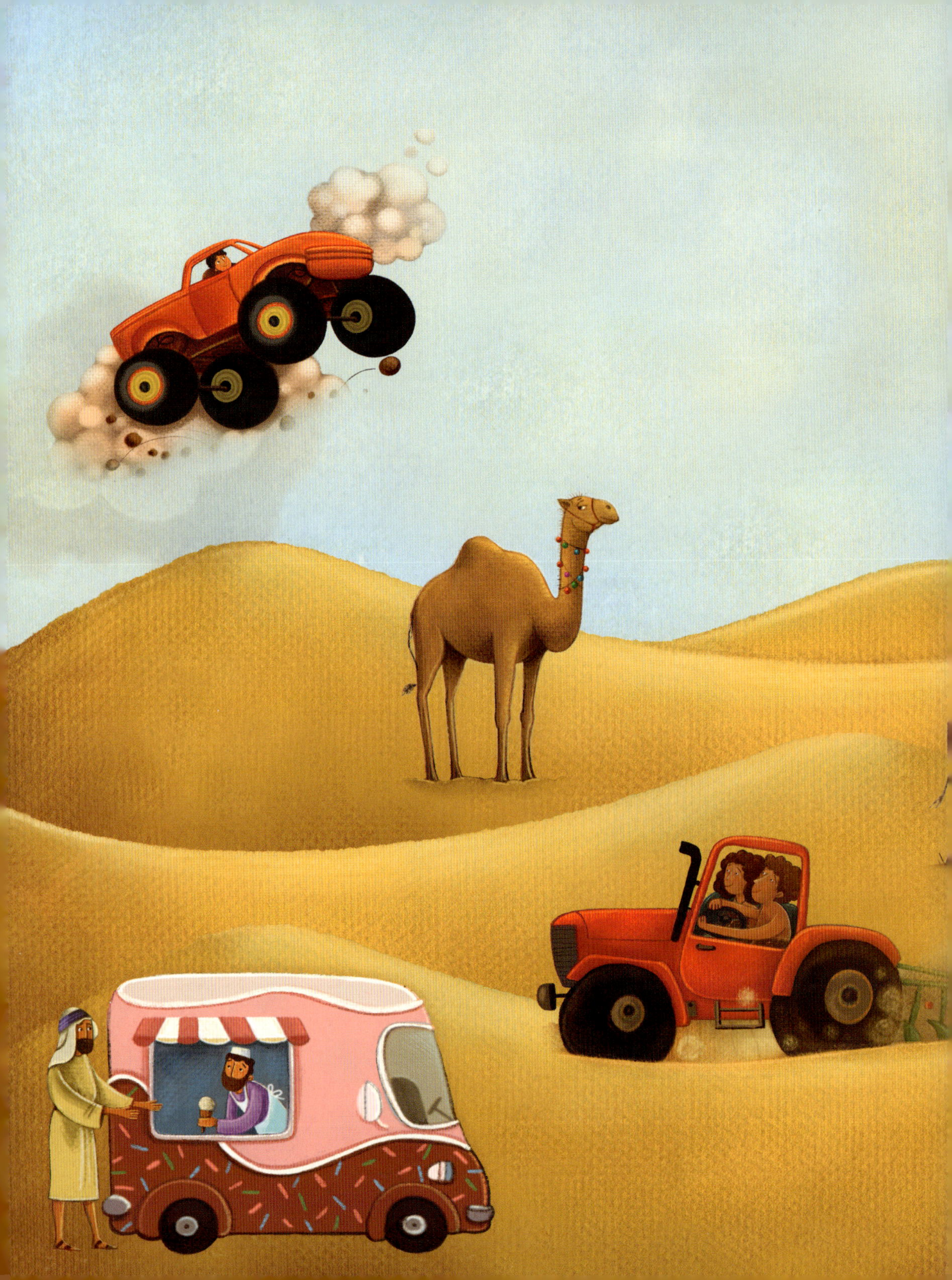

LET'S GO!

Bible Adventures

Real Bible Stories for Kids Who Love Trains, Tractors, Ice Cream Trucks, and More!

Valerie Ellis

illustrated by Carolina Farias

TYNDALE KIDS

Tyndale House Publishers
Carol Stream, Illinois

Visit Tyndale's website for kids at tyndale.com/kids.

Visit the author online at valerieellis.com

Tyndale is a registered trademark of Tyndale House Ministries. The Tyndale Kids logo is a trademark of Tyndale House Ministries.

Let's Go! Bible Adventures: Real Bible Stories for Kids Who Love Trains, Tractors, Ice Cream Trucks, and More!

Copyright © 2025 by Valerie Ellis. All rights reserved.

Illustrations copyright © Carolina Fariás. All rights reserved.

Author photo by Jennifer Brogan of Two Feet, Four Feet Photography, Copyright © 2017. All rights reserved.

Designed by Jacqueline L. Nuñez

Published in association with the literary agency of Bourland Strategic Advisors.

Scripture quotations are taken from the New American Standard Bible,® copyright © 1960, 1962, 1963, 1968, 1971, 1972, 1973, 1975, 1977, 1995 by The Lockman Foundation. Used by permission.

For manufacturing information regarding this product, please call 1-855-277-9400.

For information about special discounts for bulk purchases, please contact Tyndale House Publishers at csresponse@tyndale.com, or call 1-855-277-9400.

Library of Congress Cataloging-in-Publication Data
A catalog record for this book is available from the Library of Congress.

ISBN 978-1-4964-8148-1

Printed in China

31 30 29 28 27 26 25
7 6 5 4 3 2 1

To Gavin and Callen,

You bring me so much joy and inspiration on this amazing adventure with God. Let's go!

Contents

Old Testament

Adam and Eve 2
Noah and the Flood 6
The Tower of Babel 10
God's Call to Abraham 14
Abraham and Sarah Wait 18
Rebekah and Isaac Meet 22
Jacob and Esau Reunite 26
Joseph Saves Many Lives 30
Baby Moses 34
God Rescues the Israelites 38
Ruth and Boaz 42
Hannah and Samuel 46
David and Goliath 50
King Solomon Builds a Temple for God 54
God Provides for Elijah 58
Elijah Goes to Heaven 62
Naaman and Elisha 66
God Sends Jonah to Nineveh 70
King Josiah Gets Rid of Idols 74
Esther Speaks Up 78

New Testament

Jesus Is Born	84
God Announces Jesus' Birth	88
The Wise Men	92
John the Baptist Prepares the Way for Jesus	96
Jesus Teaches the People	100
Four Friends Bring a Man to Jesus	104
A Boy Needs Healing	108
Jesus, the Disciples, and the Storm	112
Jesus Feeds More Than 5,000 People	116
Jesus Meets the Disciples on the Water	120
Jesus and Zacchaeus	124
Jesus and Lazarus	128
Jesus Enters Jerusalem	132
Dirty Streets and Dirty Feet	136
Jesus Is Arrested	140
Jesus' Resurrection	144
Jesus Ascends into Heaven	148
God Sends the Holy Spirit	152
Philip and the Ethiopian Official	156
Paul Shares God's Love	160
Acknowledgments	*167*
About the Author	*171*

God gave us the Bible to help us see

God's love never changes—it's strong as can be!

But some things were different a long time ago,

Like how people went where they needed to go.

What did they use to work hard or go far?

Did they drive a tractor, a cruise ship, a car?

Whether through waves or on rough, rocky ground,

Let's see how they worked hard and traveled around!

Fast or slow, high or low!
We're on an adventure with God.

LET'S GO!

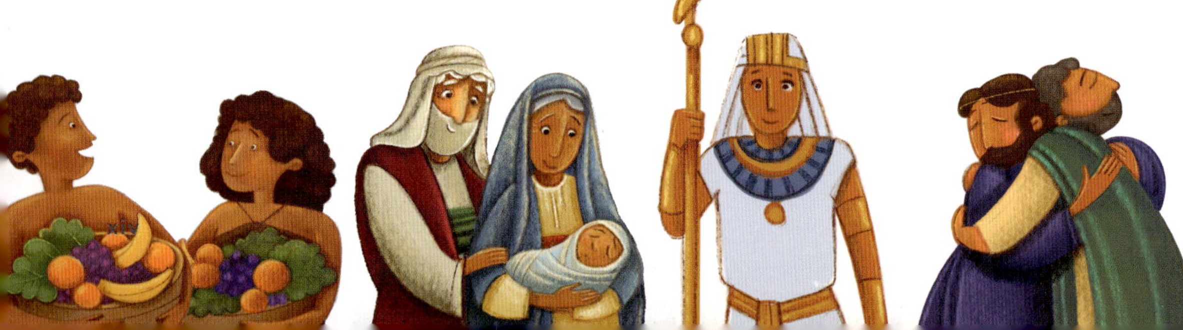

OLD TESTAMENT

When God made the world, the story began.

Each person was crafted with love in God's plan.

Their stories were woven to make God's love clear.

Ready? It's time to meet some of them here.

Adam and Eve

From Genesis 1–3

Walking with God in the garden was grand

'Til Adam and Eve disobeyed God's command.

Then planting and growing got so hard to do.

Could they use a tractor to help them get through?

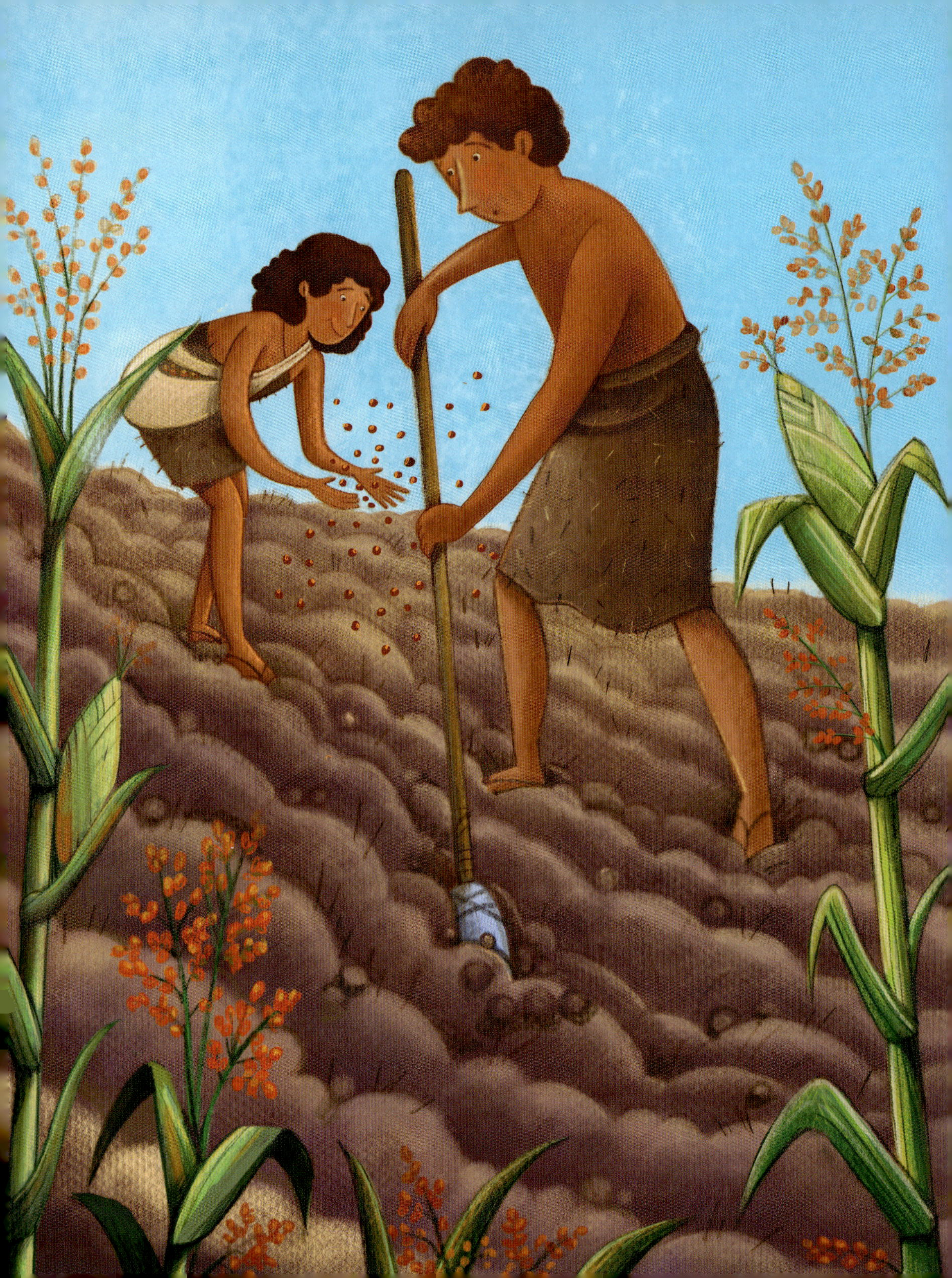

No, tractors with gears could not help plow the land.
So they used stone tools, and they farmed it by hand.
Through every mistake that they made, God stayed true,
And God, who is good, forgives our mistakes too.

What else? When Adam and Eve disobeyed God, it hurt their friendship with God and affected creation too. Even the land became harder to farm! But one thing that didn't change was God's love. God always cares for us.

God forgives us, this we know.
We're on an adventure with God.

LET'S GO!

Noah and the Flood

From Genesis 6:5–8:22

A great flood was coming, and God's heart was sad.

All people—but Noah—did nothing but bad.

To save Noah's family, the animals too,

Did God send a cruise ship? Now, what did God do?

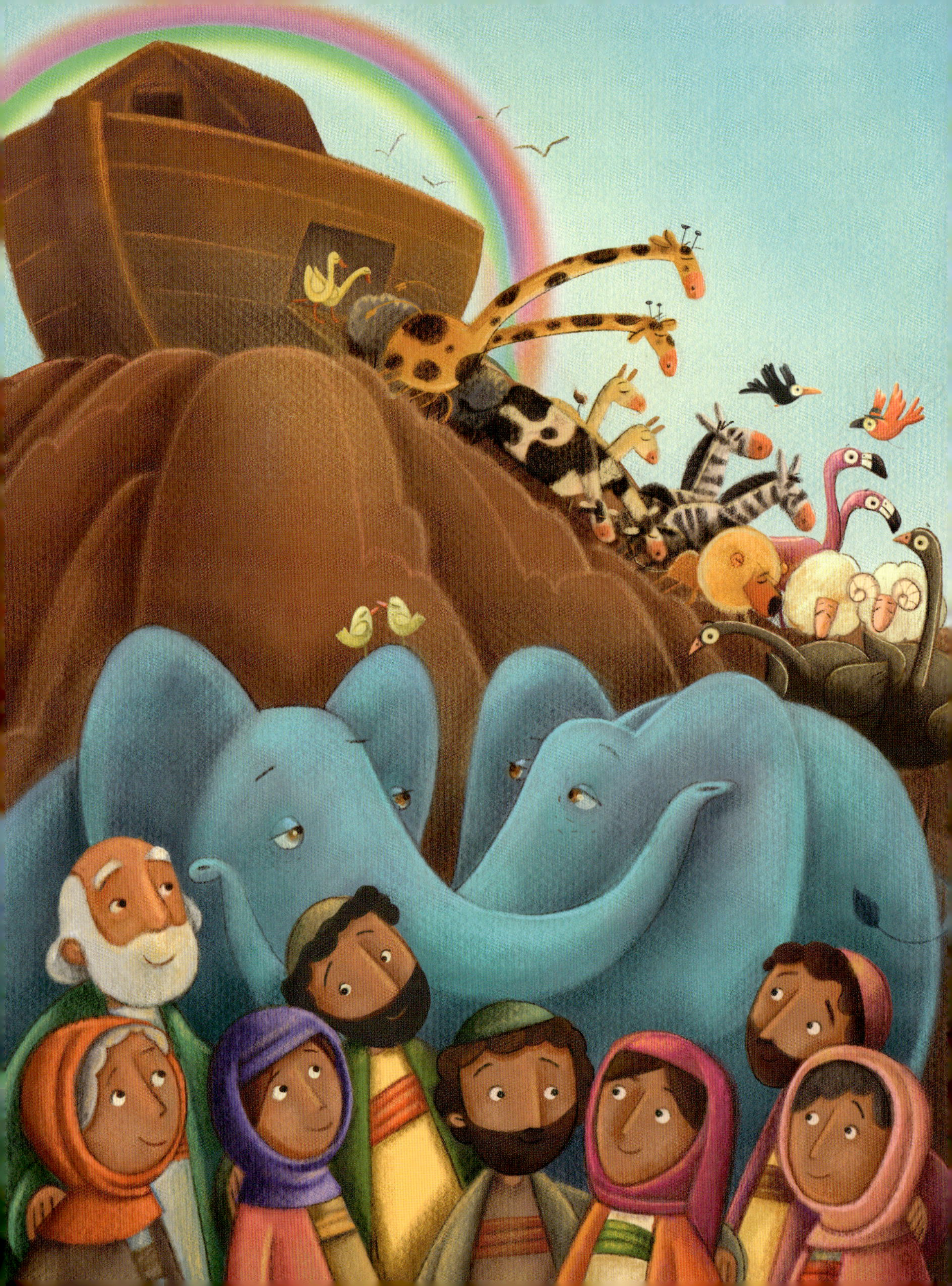

In kindness so great, God told Noah to build.
Creatures came in, and the big ark was filled.
When rain fell and waves rose, they stayed nice and dry.
Then they saw God's promise of love in the sky.

What else? The ark was huge—about as tall as three giraffes standing on each other's heads and as long as 23 elephants lined up trunk to tail.

God's love shines in the rainbow's glow.
We're on an adventure with God.

LET'S GO!

The Tower of Babel

From Genesis 11:1-9

"Nothing can stop us! We'll build to the sky,

Famous and strong in our tower so high!"

They dug down to bedrock to get the site set.

What did they use? There were no backhoes yet.

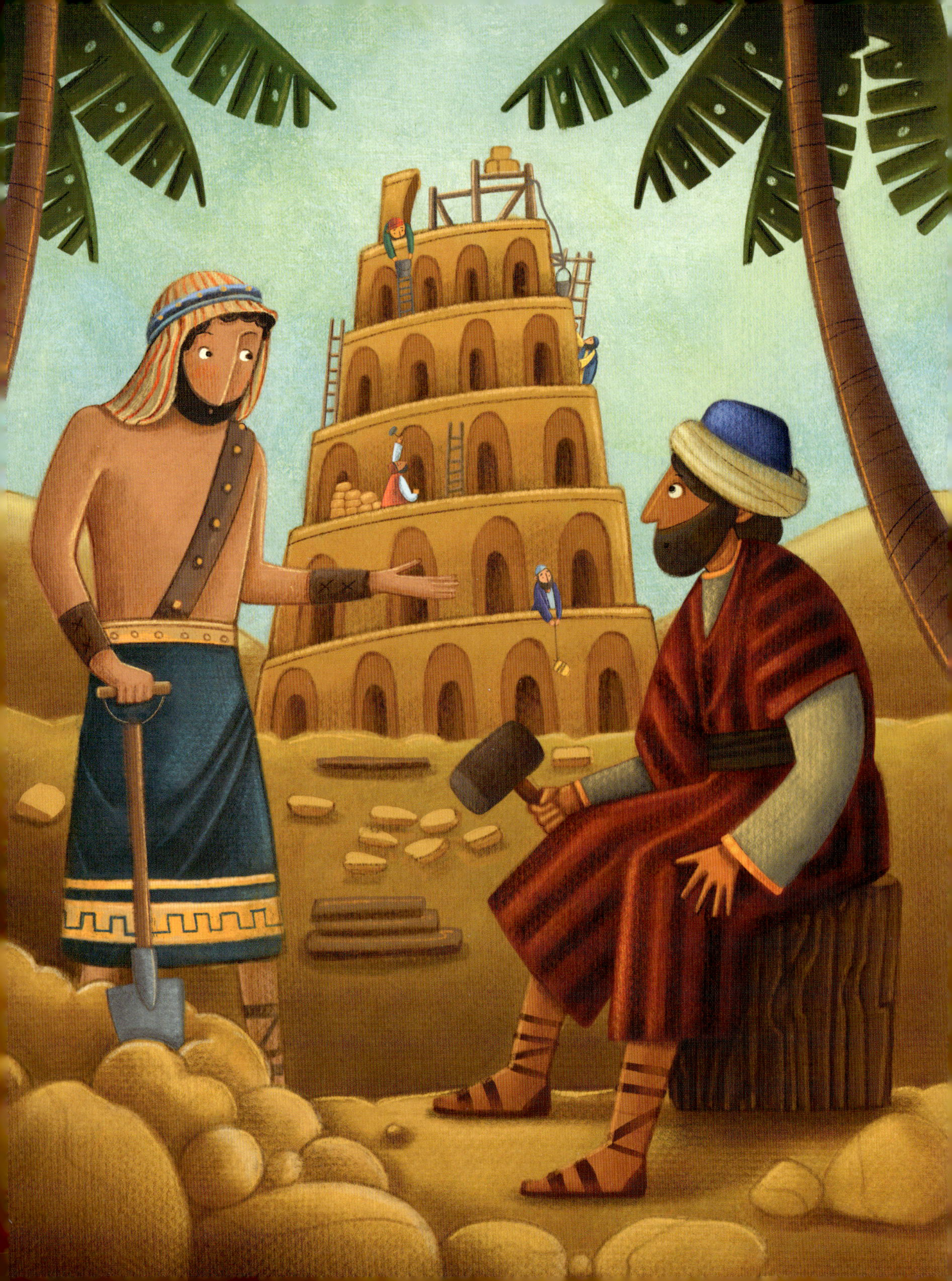

With shovels they prepped a foundation so strong,
But as they built higher, oh, something went wrong!
God mixed up their speech, so they could not proceed,
Since God—not a tower—is what people need.

What else? Before God lovingly stopped their tall-tower plans, the people stacked layer after layer of baked bricks and sticky tar.

It's God we need.
God loves us so!
We're on an adventure with God.

LET'S GO!

God's Call to Abraham

From Genesis 12:1-9

God said to Abraham, "Get up and go

To lands I will show you. Leave all that you know."

Abraham listened. He didn't complain.

Did he take a jeep through the rugged terrain?

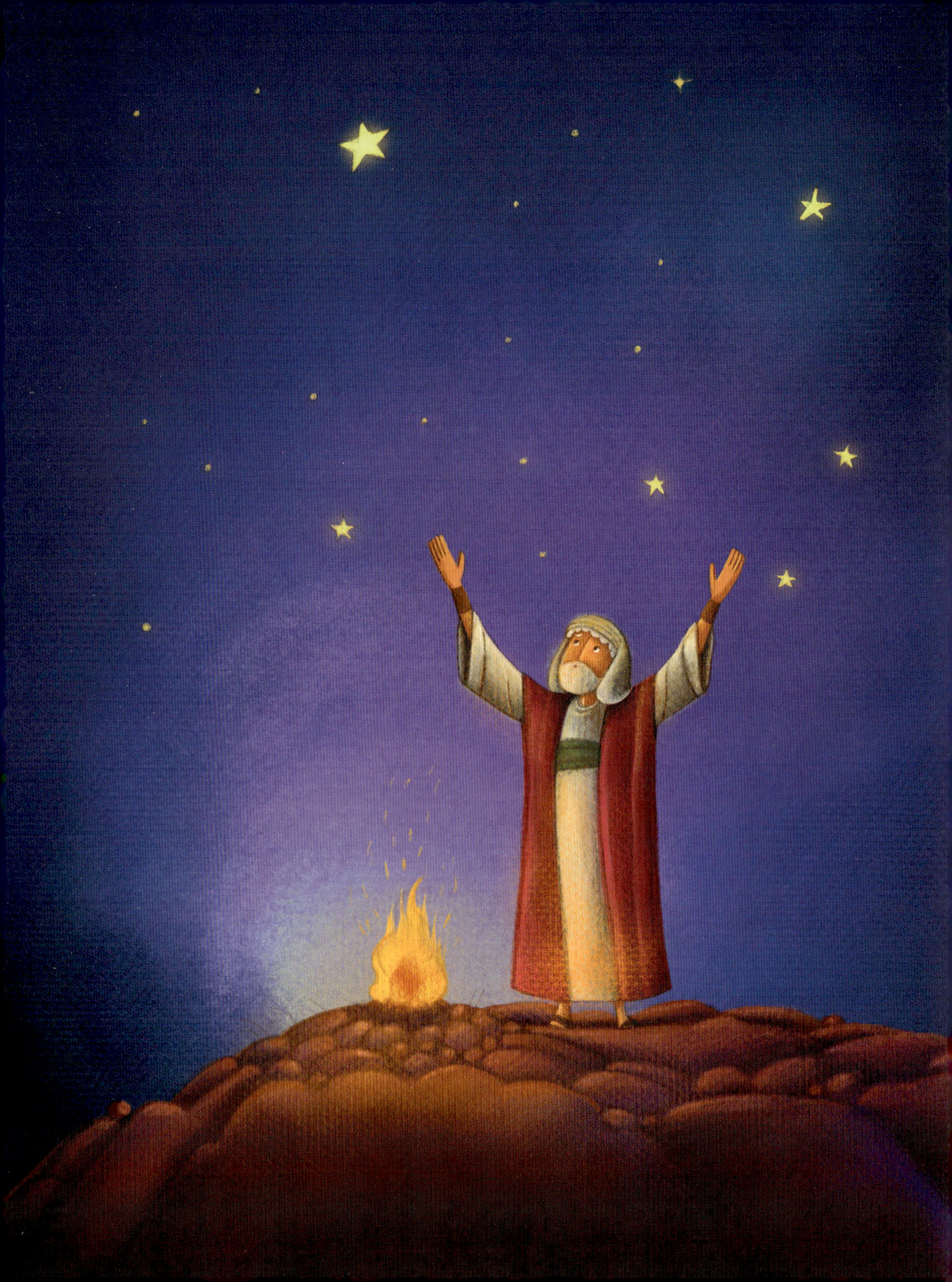

He went where God showed him and chose to believe

The promises God said he'd someday receive:

More grandchildren than the bright stars up above,

The good land God showed him, and God's awesome love.

What else? Abraham's trip would have taken less than a day by jeep, but by foot, camel, or donkey—including time to rest—it could have taken almost a month.

God points the way when we don't know.

We're on an adventure with God.

LET'S GO!

Abraham and Sarah Wait

From Genesis 18:1-15 and 21:1-3

Sarah and Abraham hoped for so long.

God promised a son—but did they hear wrong?

Though they were old, yes, their family *would* grow!

Did God send a mail truck to let them both know?

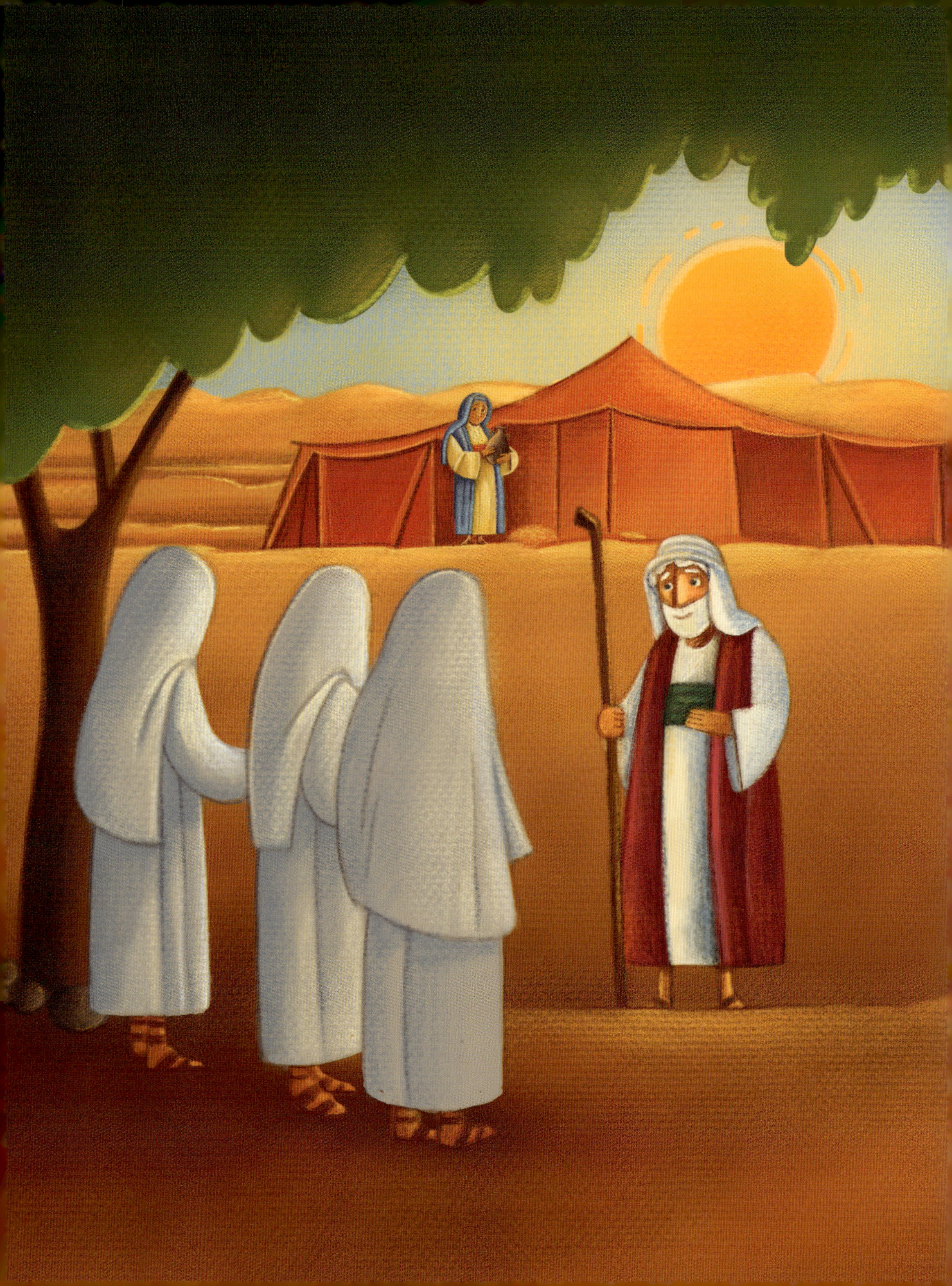

No mail truck drove up, and no letter was sent,
But heavenly messengers came to their tent.
Soon Isaac was born. Amazing, but true!
When God makes a promise, God always comes through.

What else? Sarah was 90 years old when Isaac was born, and Abraham was 100! No matter how young or old we are, God loves us.

Trust God when doubt begins to grow.
We're on an adventure with God.

LET'S GO!

Rebekah and Isaac Meet

From Genesis 24 and Matthew 1:1-2

Abraham's helper went far to find

A woman whose actions were selfless and kind.

Rebekah's big heart showed that she was the one

That God planned for Isaac, Abraham's son.

Did she take a bus on the long, dusty ride?

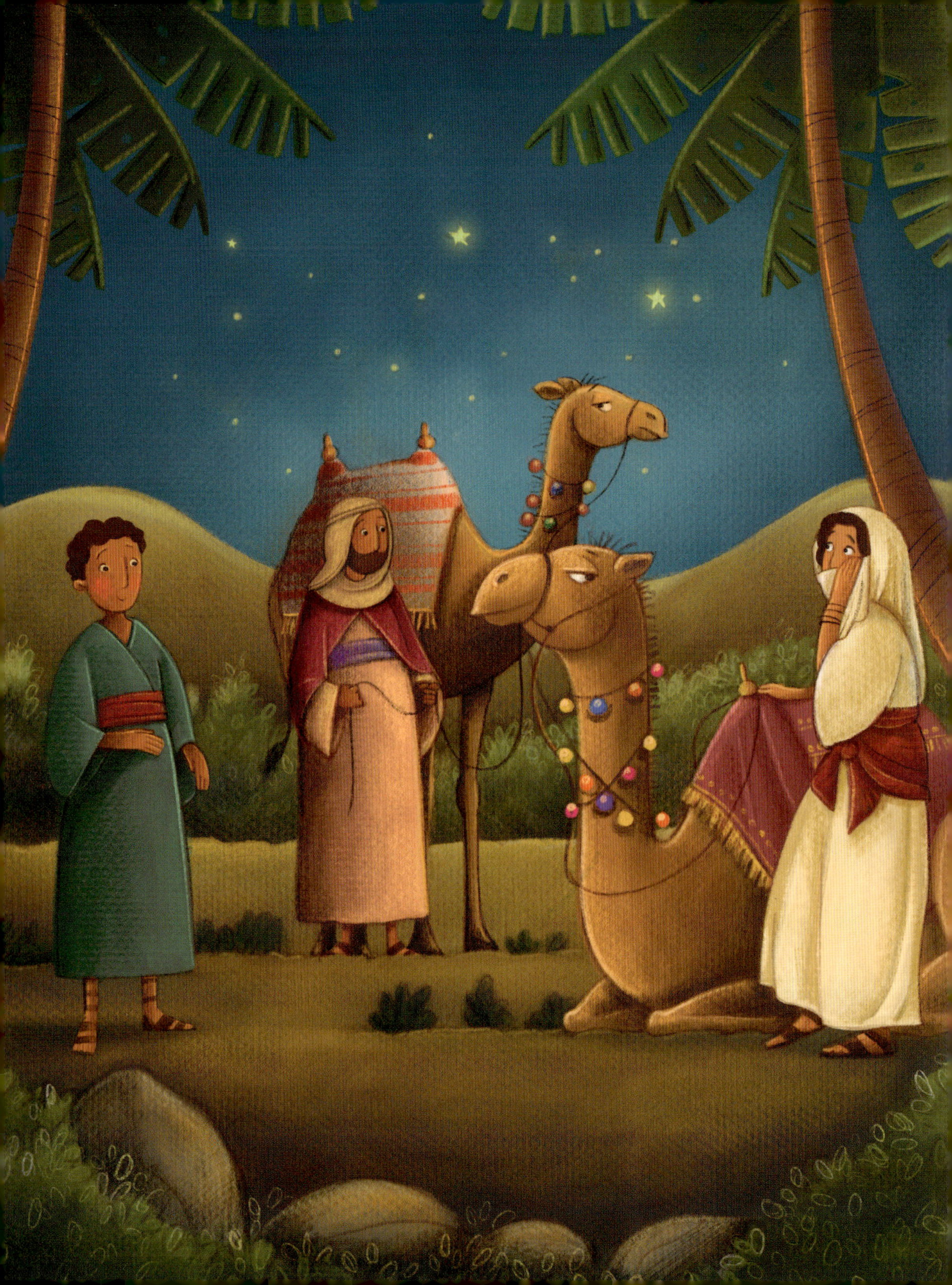

No, she rode a camel to be Isaac's bride.
As part of God's story, their small family grew
And showed to the world God's promises true.

What else? Camels can travel long distances—up to 100 miles—without water. Camels store fat in their humps, and their bodies can change that fat into water and energy when needed.

Watch God's kindness overflow!
We're on an adventure with God.

LET'S GO!

Jacob and Esau Reunite

From Genesis 32–33

Traveling home, Jacob breathed out a prayer:

"May Esau forgive me for being unfair."

How did his family traverse all that sand?

Did RVs and cattle trucks zoom through the land?

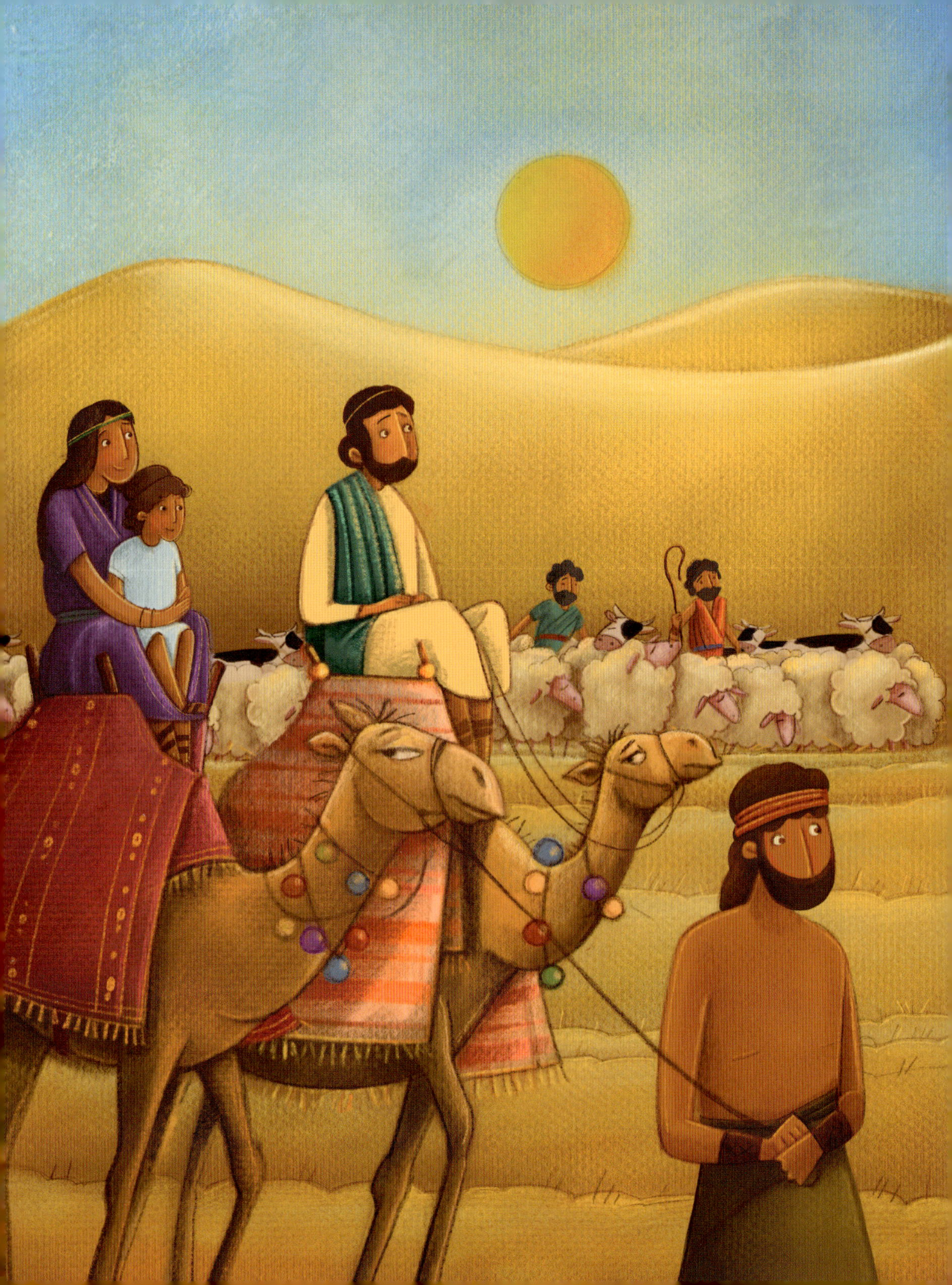

They went in a caravan, resting each night,
Unsure whether Esau intended to fight.
Esau forgave him. The brothers were friends,
Reminding us God loves when we make amends!

What else? When they were younger, Jacob cheated his brother and ran away. No wonder Jacob was worried about seeing Esau again! But Esau was so happy to be with his brother that he ran up and gave him a hug.

Forgive and let peace start to grow.

We're on an adventure with God.

LET'S GO!

Joseph Saves Many Lives
From Genesis 41:1–47:25

God gave Joseph wisdom so he could prepare

For famine in Egypt and save food to share.

His brothers were far away—hungry and sad.

Did they come by van with their kids and their dad?

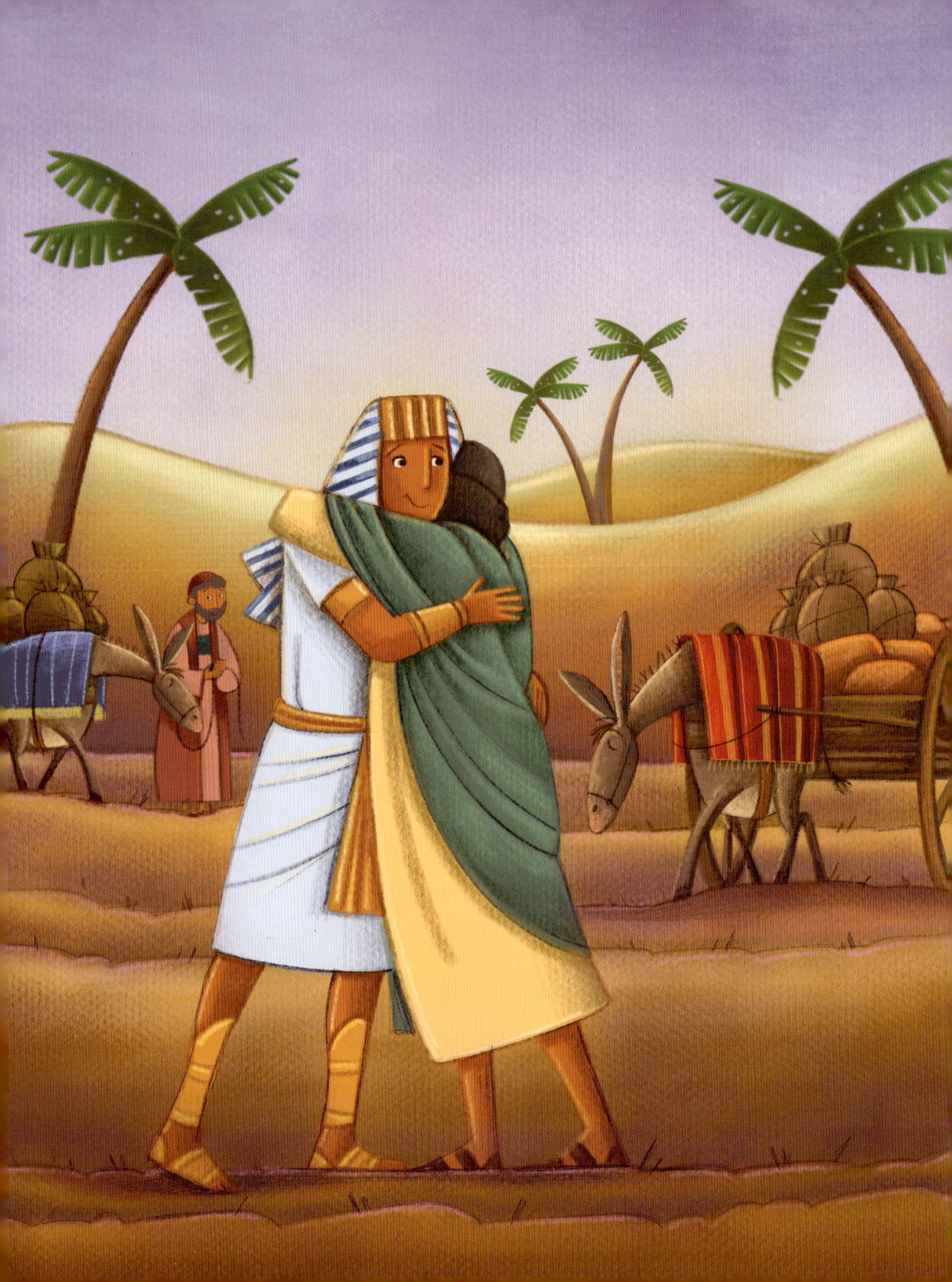

With donkeys and carts, they all moved to be near
To Joseph, who'd care for them year after year.
God was so faithful and helped Joseph shine
To save many lives by the Lord's grand design.

What else? People came to Egypt from far and wide to buy the grain Joseph had wisely stored up. Grain was often ground into flour to bake bread.

Share God's goodness.
Let love flow.
We're on an adventure with God.

LET'S GO!

Baby Moses
From Exodus 1:1–2:10

Egypt's new king was demanding and rough,

Hurting God's people and making life tough—

Even for babies! Where could Moses hide?

Did Mom find a life raft and place him inside?

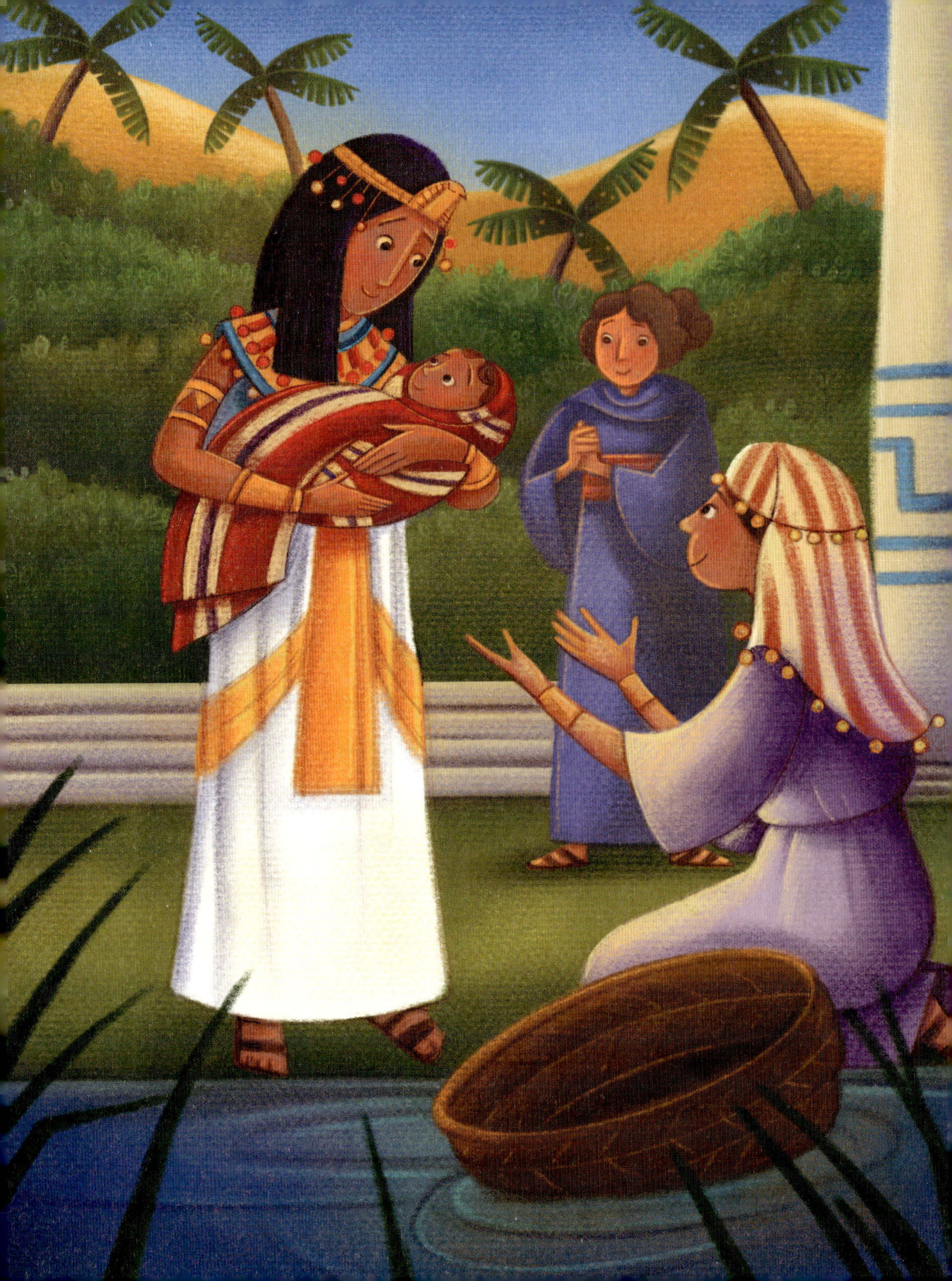

To save baby Moses, a basket was made.

His sister watched closely. It bobbed in the shade.

God used the king's daughter to rescue this son.

Soon God would work wonders to free everyone.

What else? In ancient Egypt, kings were called pharaohs. Moses grew up to lead God's people out of Egypt and away from the cruel pharaoh.

God will use the love we show.

We're on an adventure with God.

LET'S GO!

God Rescues the Israelites

From Exodus 14:5–15:21 and Micah 6:4

Following Moses, God's people were free.

They fled Pharaoh's anger. They reached the Red Sea.

Did ferry boats take them, their cattle and sheep?

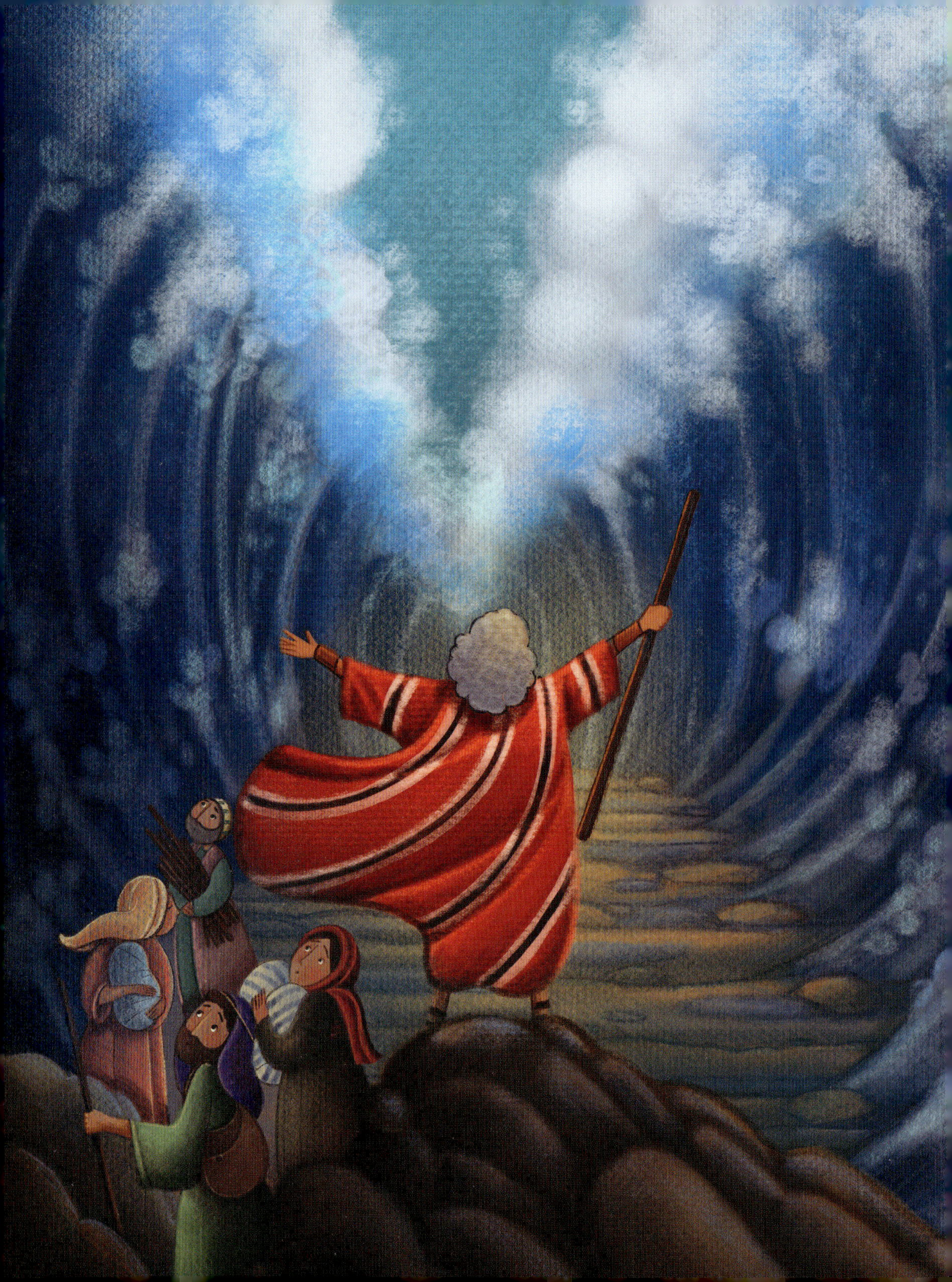

No, God made a way through the water so deep!
God parted the water, exposing the sand,
And God's people walked right across on dry land.
Then tambourines sounded at Miriam's lead
With thanks for the freedom that God guaranteed!

What else? God miraculously moved water out of the way three more times in the Bible—one time for Joshua and the Israelites, one time for Elijah, and one time for Elisha—all at the Jordan River!

Through every high and every low,
We're on an adventure with God.

LET'S GO!

Ruth and Boaz

From Ruth 1–4

"Let's harvest the barley. It's time!" Boaz said.

"We'll thresh, mix, and bake it for round loaves of bread."

No combine to harvest the stalks from the ground . . .

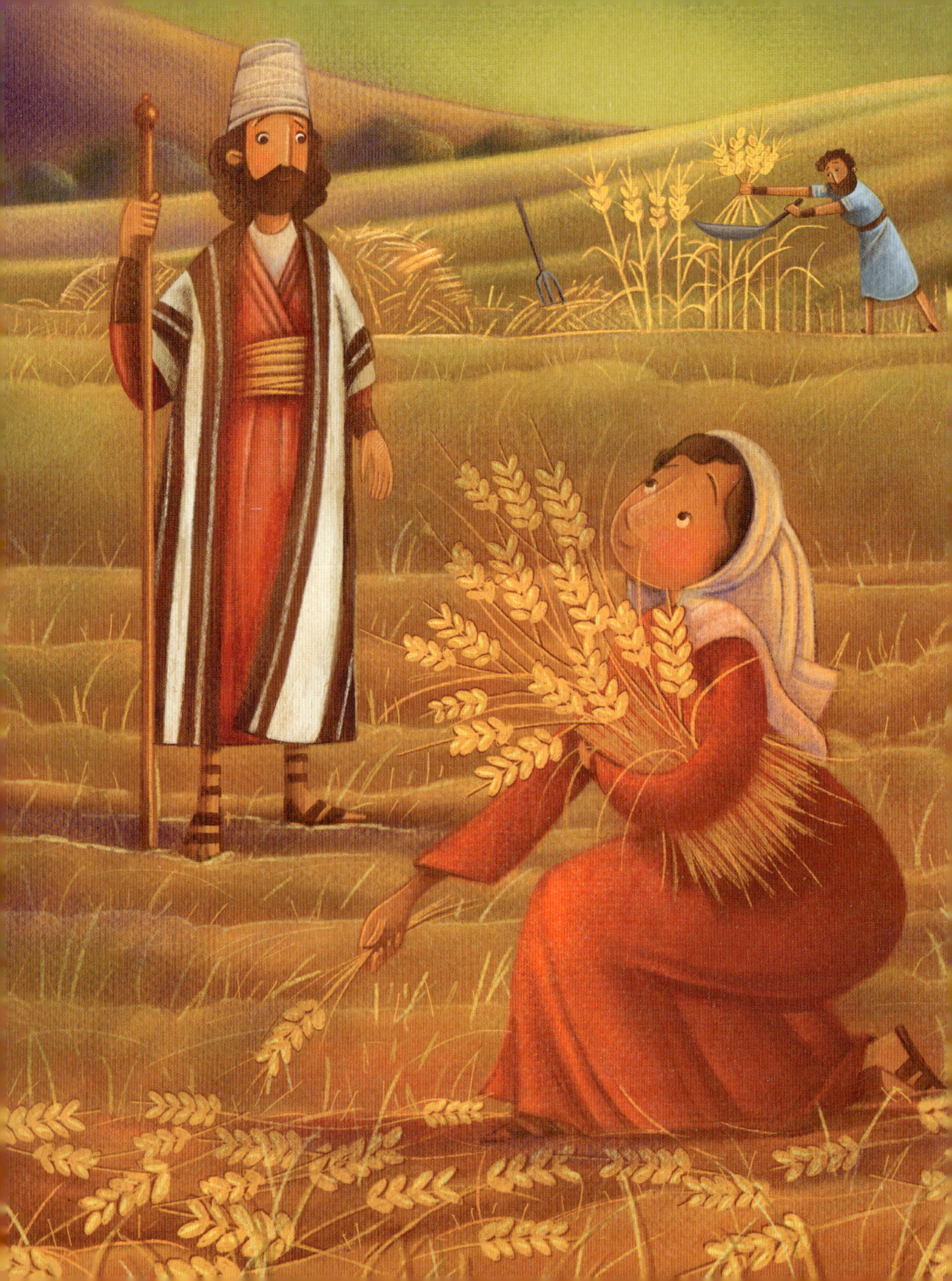

They cut it by hand, and some fell all around.

Ruth needed food, and Boaz was kind.

He said, "Let Ruth gather the grain left behind."

God gave Ruth a family, protection, and friends.

Through good times and hard times, God's love never ends.

What else? Ruth and Boaz got married, and one of their great-grandsons was King David. That means they are in Jesus' family line too!

Always trust God's love and know:
We're on an adventure with God.

LET'S GO!

Hannah and Samuel

From 1 Samuel 1

Hannah prayed hard for a sweet baby boy.

God gave her Samuel and filled her with joy!

When she took him up to the house of the Lord,

Did she ride her bike with the son she adored?

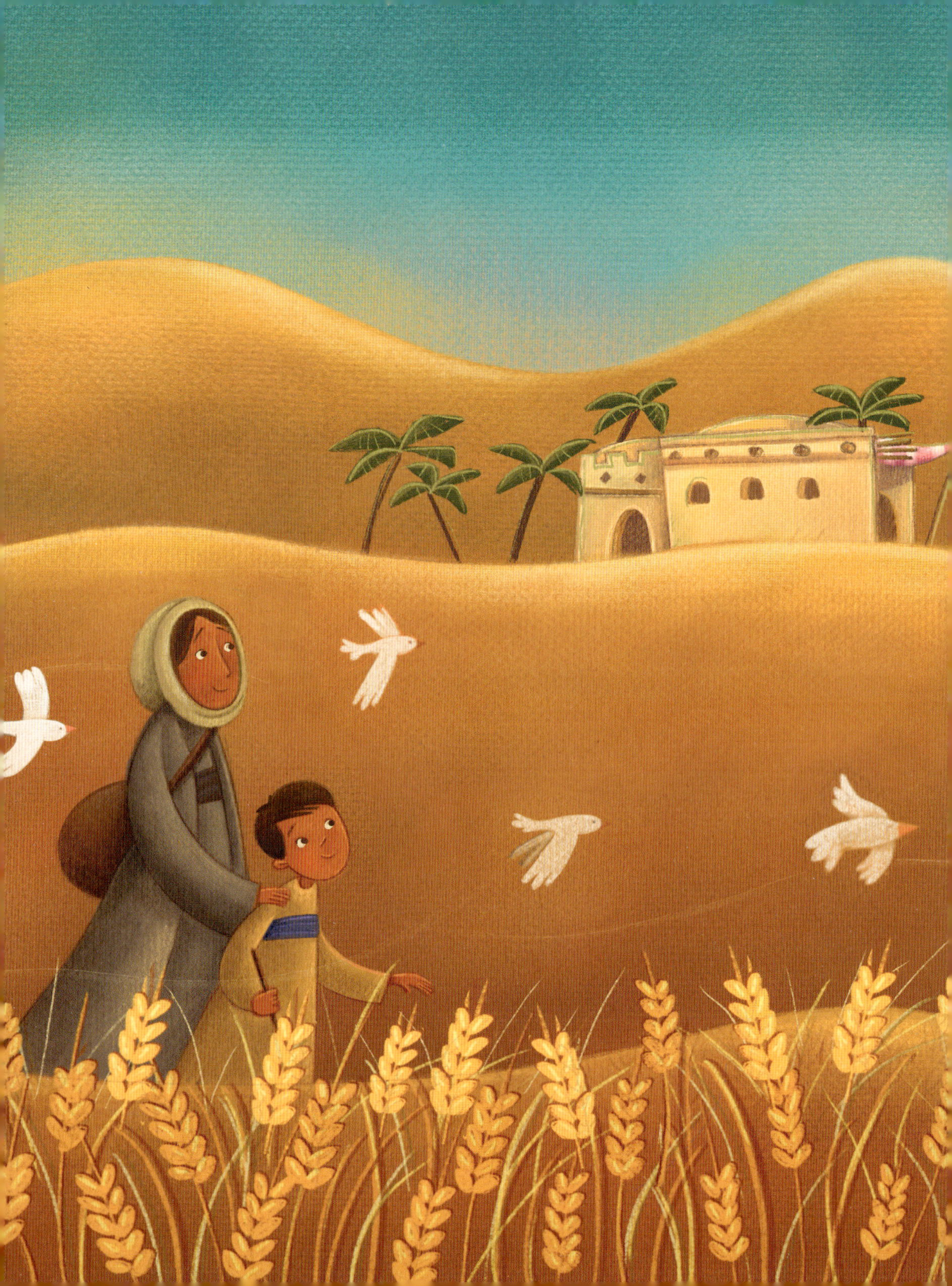

There weren't any bikes, so they walked on the sand.

Samuel would serve his whole life as God planned:

Bringing God's messages, sharing God's ways,

Encouraging people to give the Lord praise.

What else? When Samuel was a young boy living in the house of the Lord, something special happened: he heard God call his name and obeyed God's voice.

Pray to God who loves you so.
We're on an adventure with God.

LET'S GO!

David and Goliath

From 1 Samuel 17:1-50

Goliath the champion wanted to fight.

"None of God's people can match my great might!"

David was small, but he was not scared!

Did he drive a monster truck, strong and prepared?

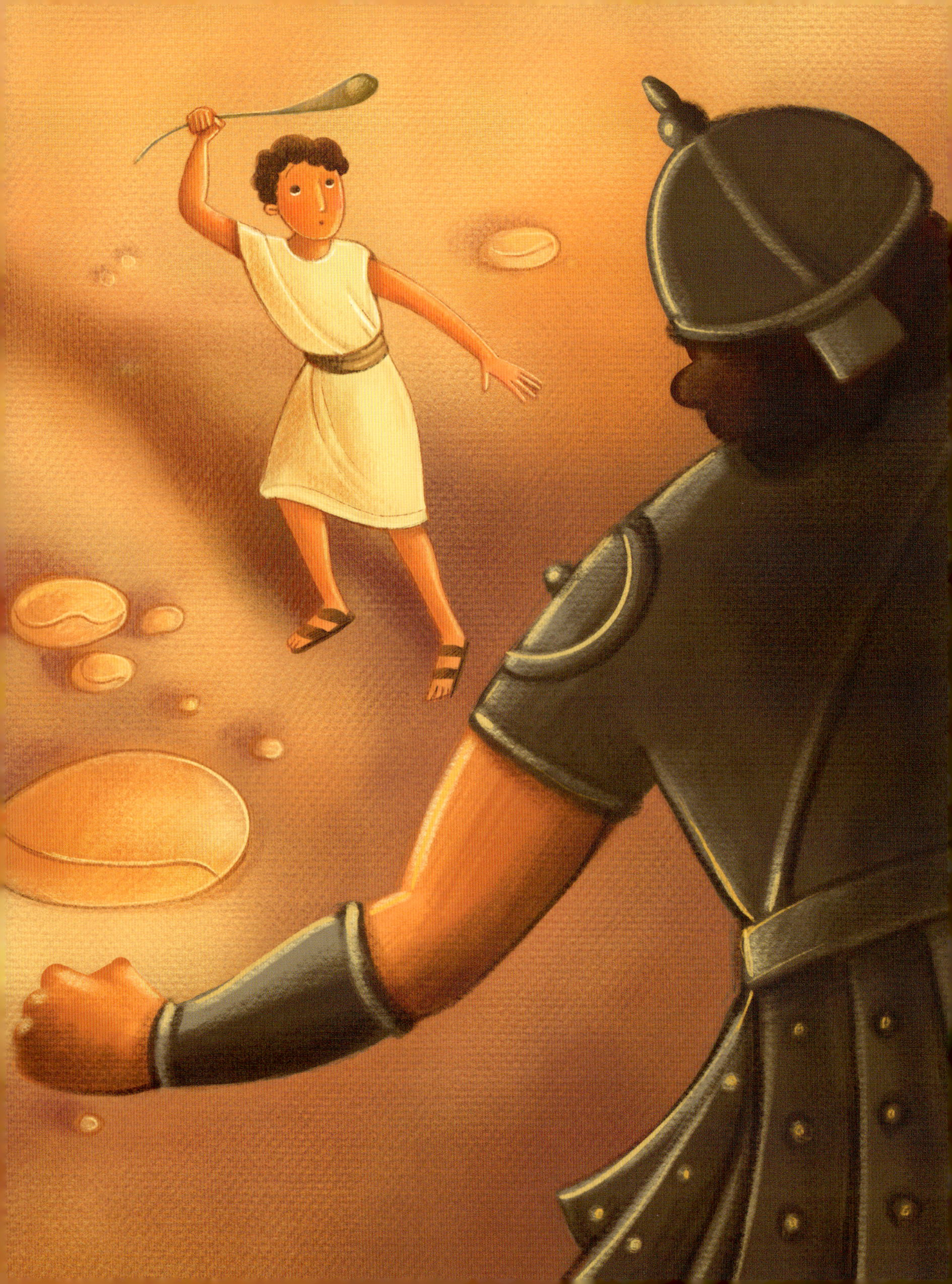

He trusted in God, not a truck, not a shield.

He won with a sling and a stone in that field.

David went on to be Israel's king.

He prayed to the Lord and wrote praises to sing.

What else? Though people did not have monster trucks in Bible times, they did have armor, helmets, and shields. But David wasn't used to all of that. He trusted in God to protect him and help him.

Trust in God and you will know:

We're on an adventure with God.

LET'S GO!

King Solomon Builds a Temple for God

From 1 Kings 5–8

Solomon's task from the Lord was to build

A temple for worship. God's people were thrilled.

He called for long timbers and gold shining bright.

Did semitrucks haul all that stuff to the site?

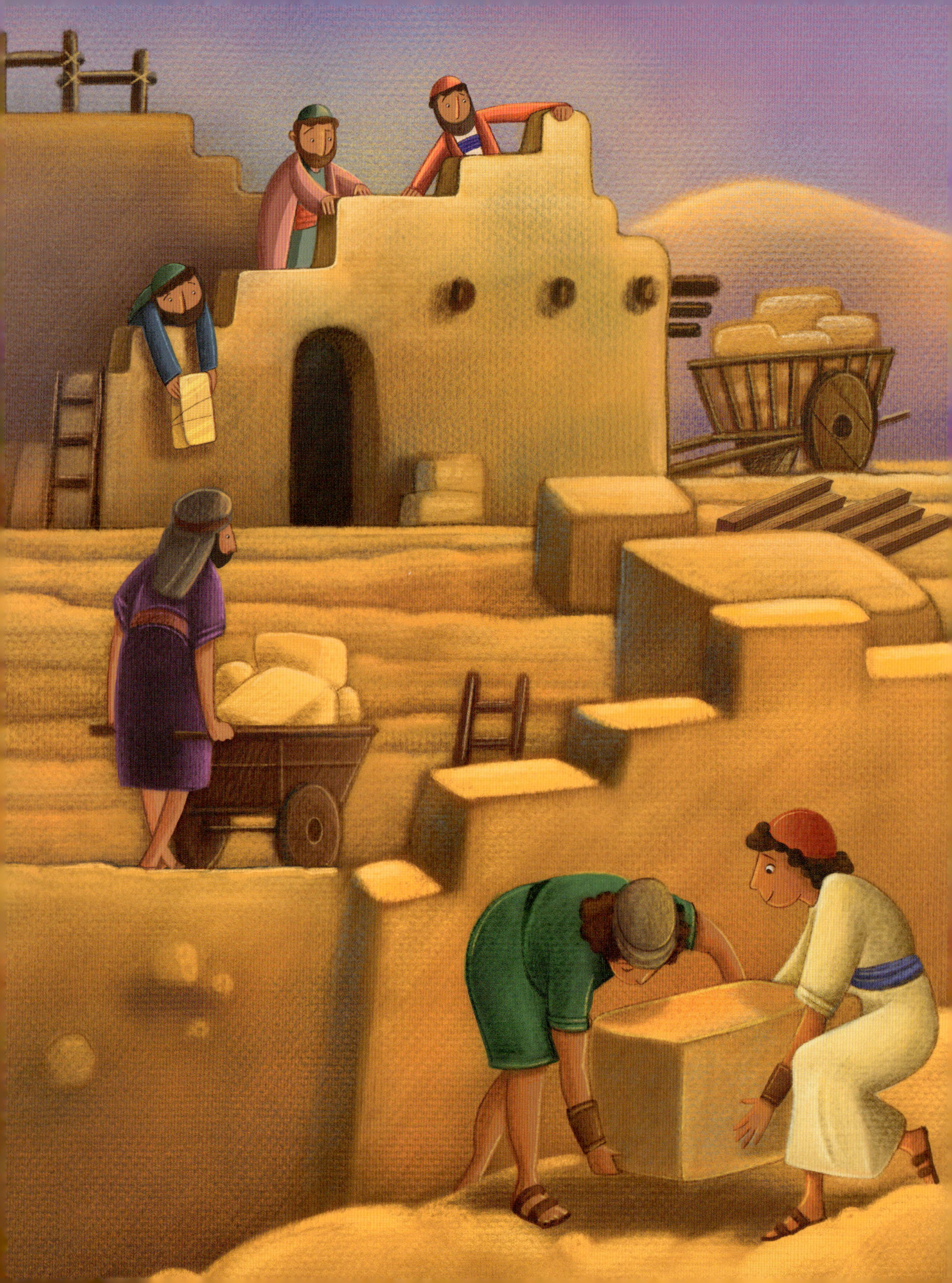

Workers prepared all the stone and the wood,

Then hauled it on wagons as fast as they could.

When God's house was finished, King Solomon prayed

That all would know God at this temple he'd made.

What else? The temple was a very special place—even while it was being built! To make sure no iron tools would be heard banging or scraping, workers prepared the stone *before* they hauled it to the construction site.

**Praise the Lord!
Let God's love show!
We're on an adventure with God.**

LET'S GO!

God Provides for Elijah

From 1 Kings 16:29-33 and 17:1-6

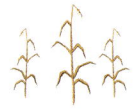

The bad things King Ahab did piled up so high,

God held back the rain and the whole land was dry.

Elijah, God's messenger, what would he eat?

Did God send an ice cream truck just for a treat?

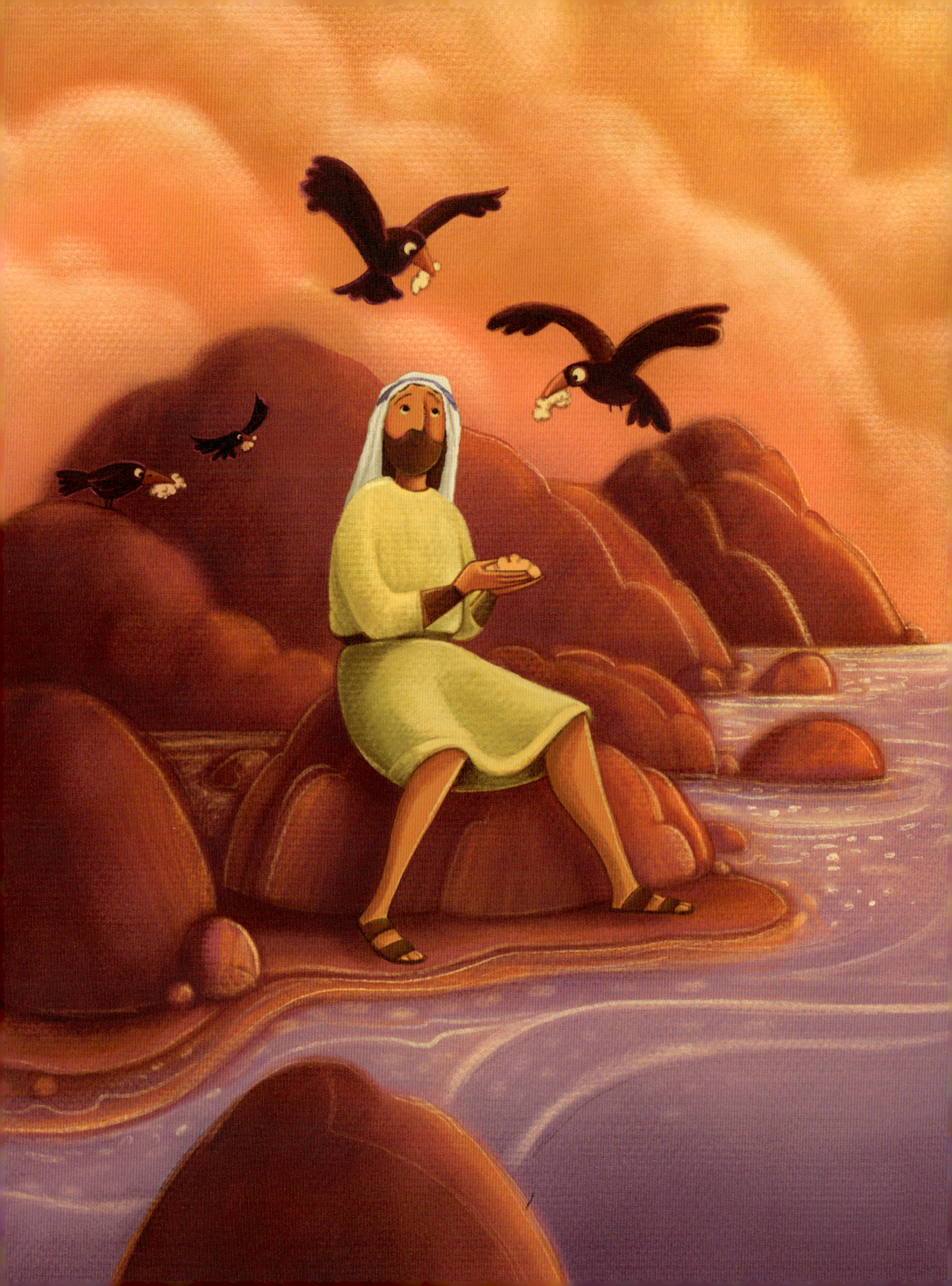

God told Elijah, "I'll keep you well-fed."

Then ravens flew over to bring meat and bread.

Elijah did wonders to help people see

The Lord is the true God who loves endlessly.

What else? After this, God fed Elijah and a small family by providing a jar of oil and a jug of flour that miraculously never ran out. When the time was right, Elijah prayed, and God sent rain.

God cares for us from head to toe.

We're on an adventure with God.

LET'S GO!

Elijah Goes to Heaven

From 2 Kings 2:1-15

Elijah the prophet served God for so long,

Speaking the truth with a passion so strong.

He'd go straight to heaven—amazing but true!

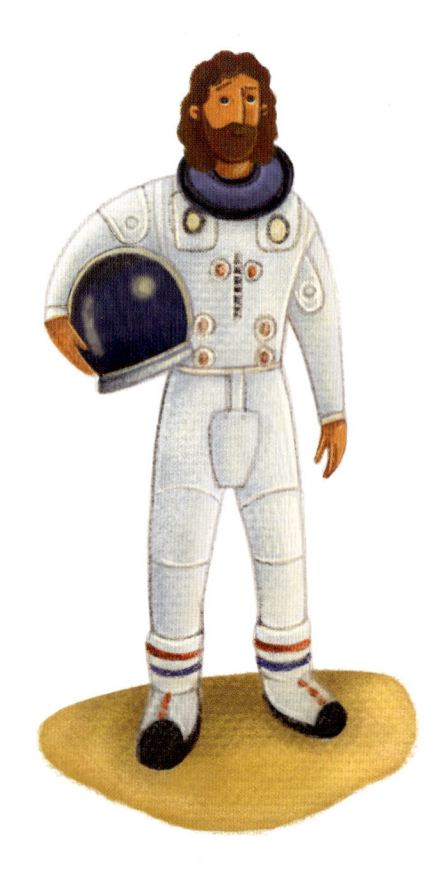

Did he take a rocket and astronaut crew?

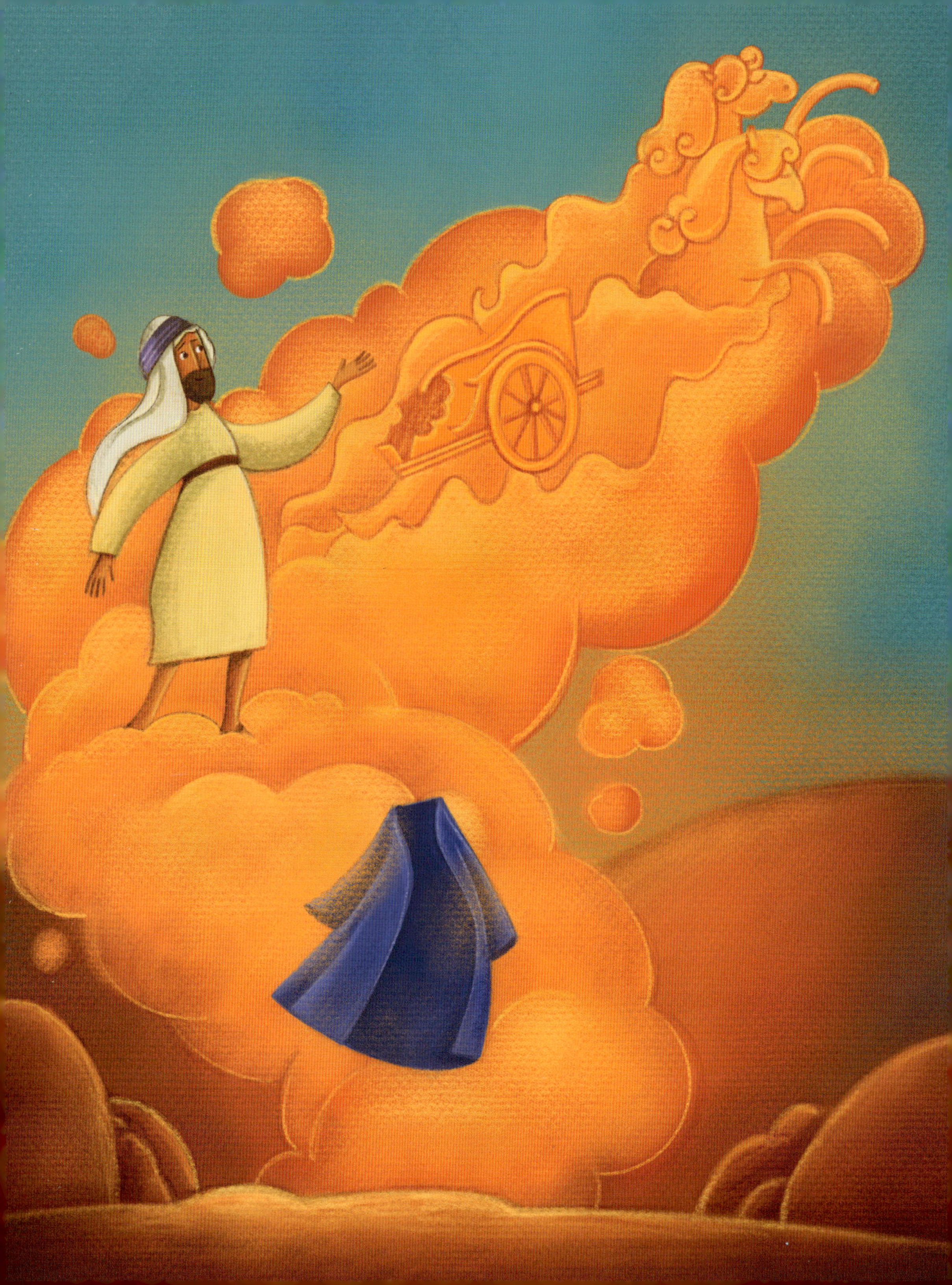

There weren't any rocket ships back in that day.

You can't soar to heaven like that anyway!

A fiery chariot came down so fast,

And mighty winds whooshed him to heaven at last!

What else? Have you ever seen horses soar from heaven? Elijah's friend, Elisha, watched the whole thing! Then he continued Elijah's work: healing, helping, and displaying God's truth in miraculous ways.

God's ways are higher than we know.

We're on an adventure with God.

LET'S GO!

Naaman and Elisha

From 2 Kings 5:1-19

Naaman was sick, and he needed a cure.

God's servant Elisha could heal him for sure.

With helpers and gifts, Naaman had to go far,

But there were no trains to pull car after car.

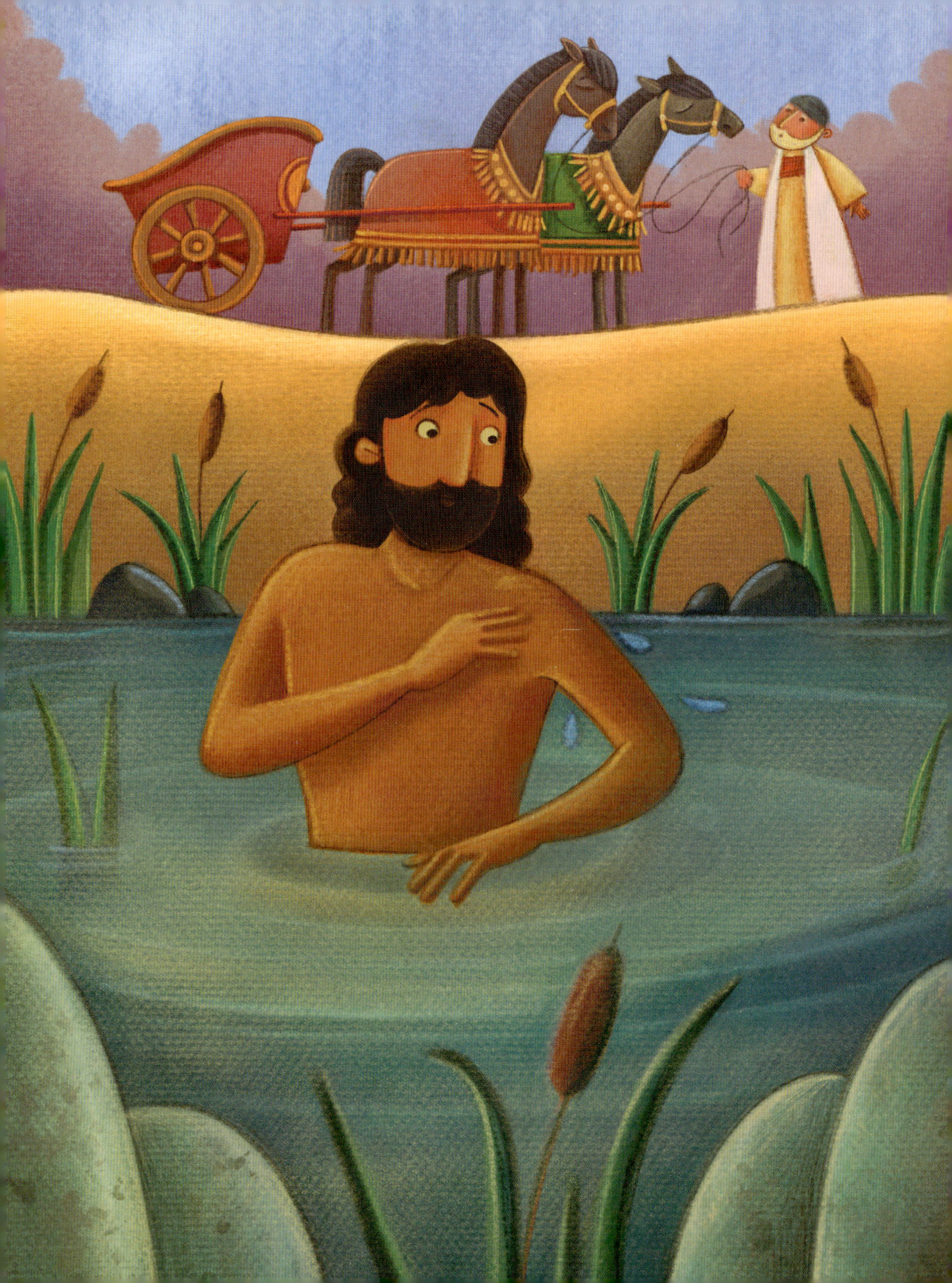

With horses and chariots, he found the right place.

Though stubborn and proud, he discovered God's grace.

The Lord God healed Naaman, his body and heart.

Naaman was thankful and made a fresh start.

What else? Naaman's chariots carried so many gifts: 750 pounds of silver, 150 pounds of gold, and 10 sets of clothing. But Elisha did not accept any of it! He gave all the glory to God instead.

God can help us change and grow.

We're on an adventure with God.

LET'S GO!

God Sends Jonah to Nineveh

From Jonah 1–4

Jonah heard God, but he did not obey.

He sailed for Tarshish, the opposite way.

A storm threatened Jonah—huge wave after wave!

Did God send a submarine, diving to save?

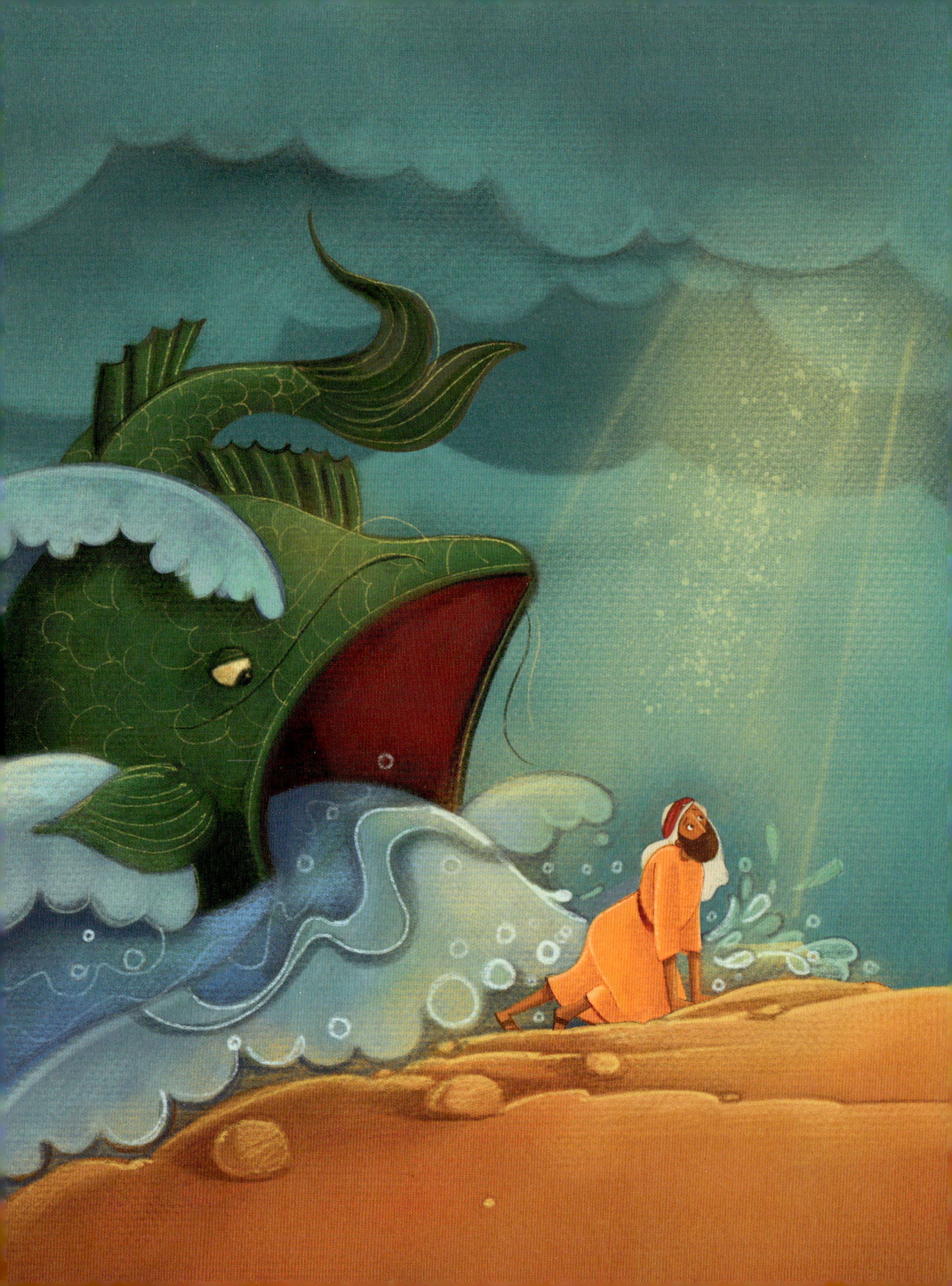

"Big fish to the rescue!" was God's kind command,

And after three days, Jonah stood on dry land.

He went off to Nineveh spreading the news

That God's path is best—it's the right one to choose.

What else? In Nineveh, Jonah spread God's message to more than 120,000 people, and they all believed!

Let's follow God.
Say yes! Not no.
We're on an adventure with God.

LET'S GO!

King Josiah Gets Rid of Idols

From 2 Kings 23:1-4

When hearts true to God could so rarely be found

And altars to false gods were built all around,

Josiah said, "All these bad things cannot stay!"

Did garbage trucks clear them and take them away?

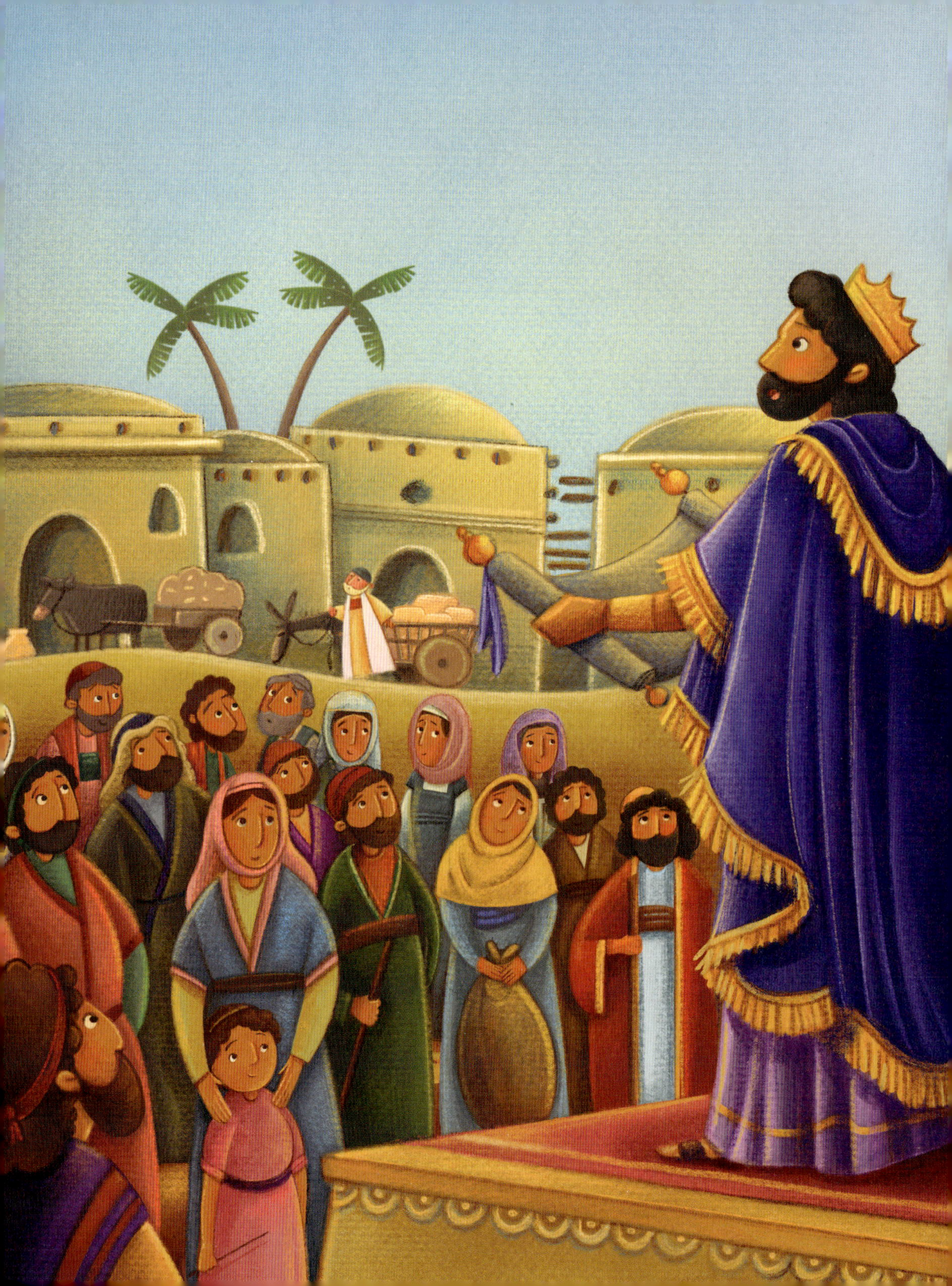

No, oxen and carts hauled the things that weren't good.

Then all in the land worshiped God as they should.

Josiah the king let God's Word be his light,

Serving with all of his heart, soul, and might.

What else? Josiah was just eight years old when he became king.

Our love and praise
to God we owe.

We're on an adventure with God.

LET'S GO!

Esther Speaks Up

From Esther 3–5 and 8

God chose Queen Esther to speak up and save

All of God's people. She had to be brave.

She asked the king, and he sent a decree—

But not by police cars as fast as can be!

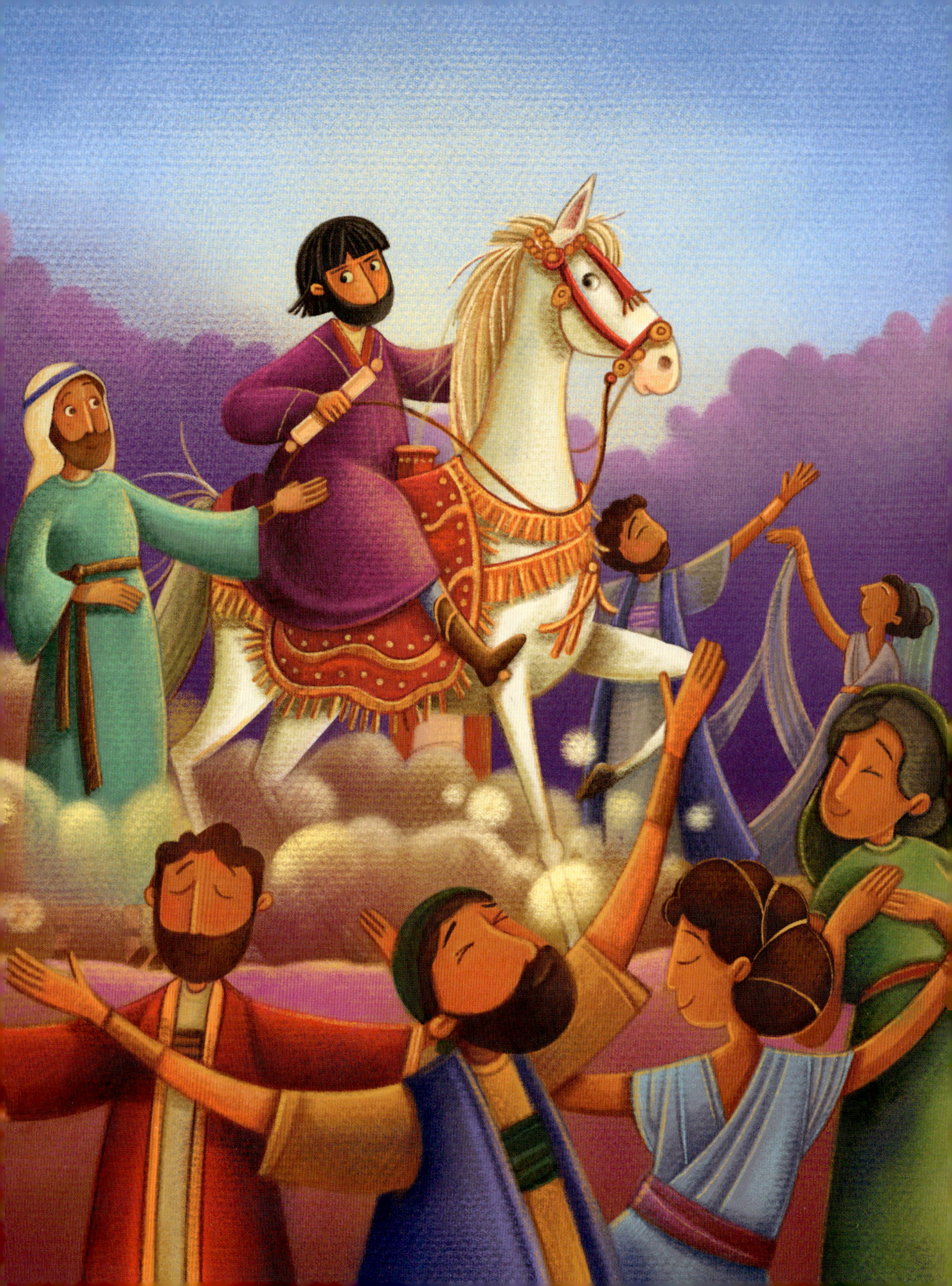

No—horses and messengers brought the good news.
God used the king's order to rescue the Jews!
Although Esther's problem seemed too big to face,
The Lord gave her wisdom and patience and grace.

What else? The king's order was urgent, so the messengers didn't take just *any* horses. They rode fast horses trained at the king's royal stables.

Trust the Lord who loves you so.
We're on an adventure with God.

LET'S GO!

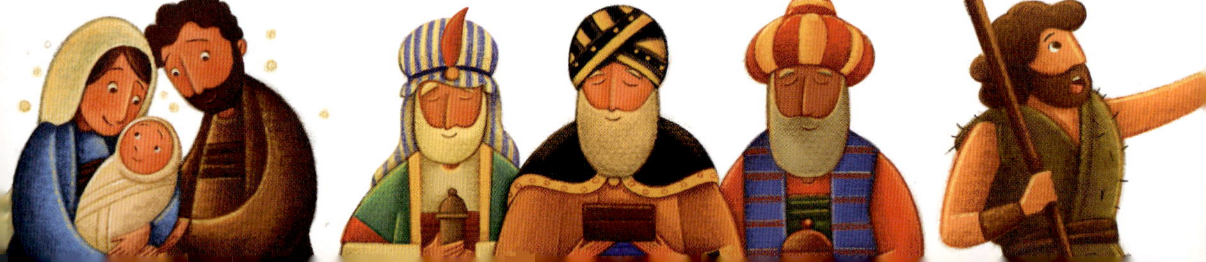

NEW TESTAMENT

Jesus Is Born

From Luke 1–2

The angel said Mary would soon have a Son,

Jesus the Savior—God's promised one!

Then Joseph said, "Let's go to Bethlehem town."

How did they go? Did they drive a car down?

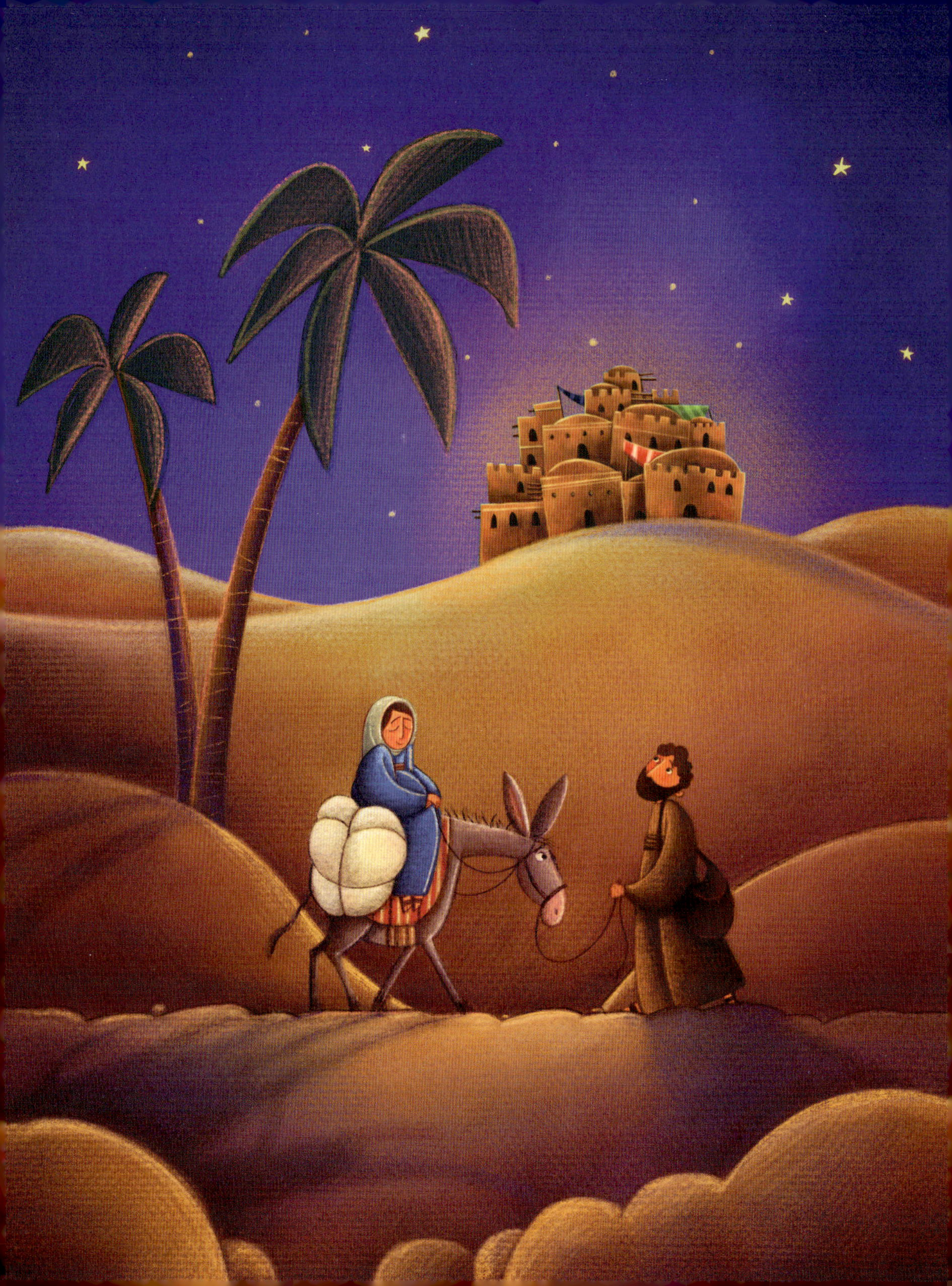

A strong, sturdy donkey gave Mary a lift.

Then Jesus was born—God's most wonderful gift!

He left heaven's wonders, His throne up above,

To bring grace and truth and to show us God's love.

What else? Hundreds of years earlier, God told people the strong, caring king they had been waiting for would be born in Bethlehem. It was Jesus!

Jesus came,
God's love to show.
We're on an adventure with God.

LET'S GO!

God Announces Jesus' Birth

From Luke 2:8-20

Jesus was born as God's gift to the earth.

Now, time to share this miraculous birth!

But *how* did our God spread a message so grand?

With banner planes soaring up over the land?

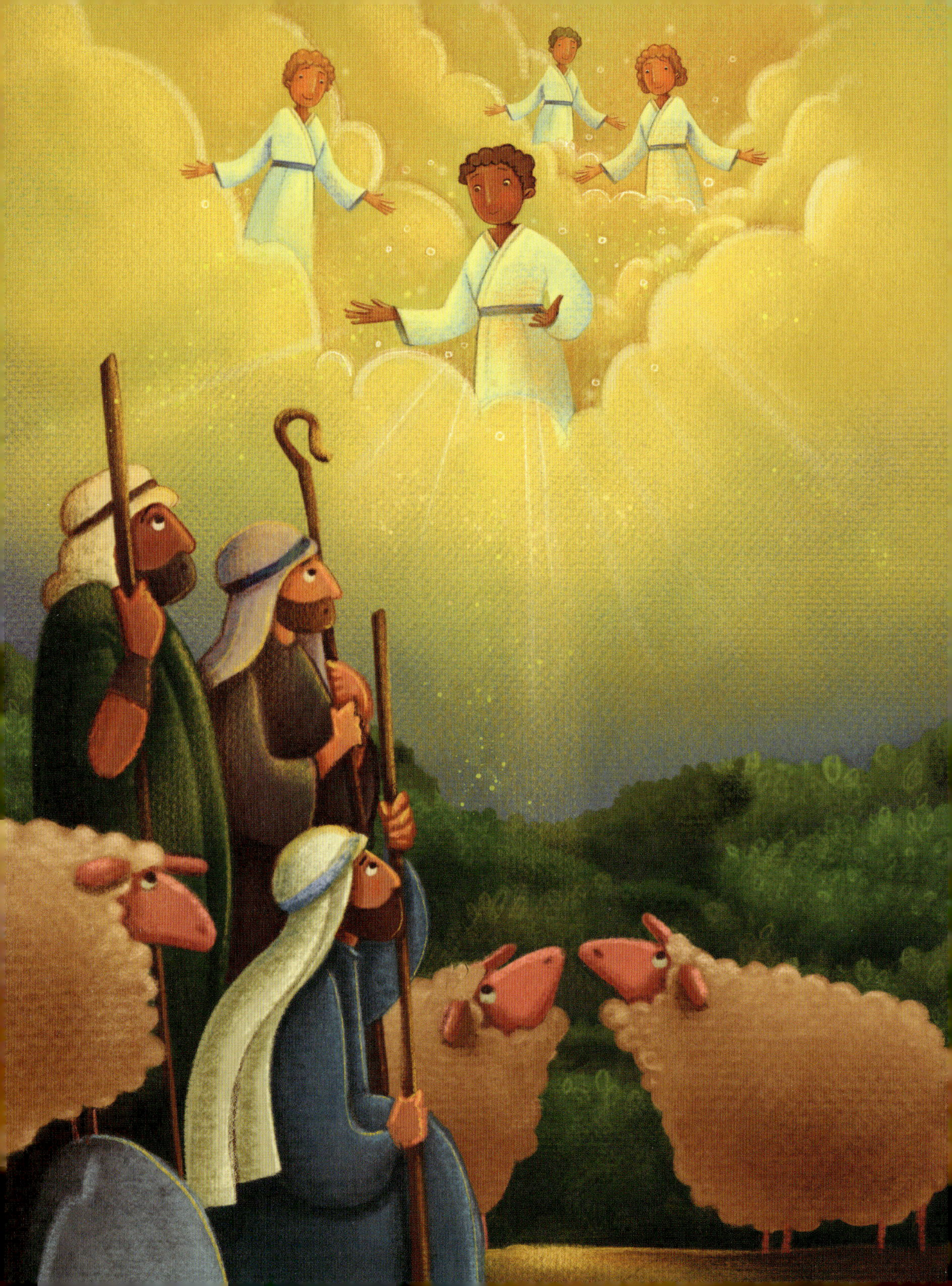

Angels and more angels filled up the sky,

Proclaiming to shepherds the babe was nearby.

The shepherds ran quickly to worship God's Son,

Then praised God and hurried to tell everyone!

What else? The shepherds weren't the only ones to run with excitement because of Jesus. Later, people ran to Jesus to be healed, to ask questions, and just to see Him. When Jesus rose from the dead, His friends ran to share the amazing news.

With Jesus, joy will overflow!

We're on an adventure with God.

LET'S GO!

The Wise Men

From Matthew 2:1-12

Wise men had presents for Jesus the King—

Gold, myrrh, and frankincense, ready to bring.

But they lived so far—wow, that trip would be hard!

Maybe just ship the gifts? Send Him a card?

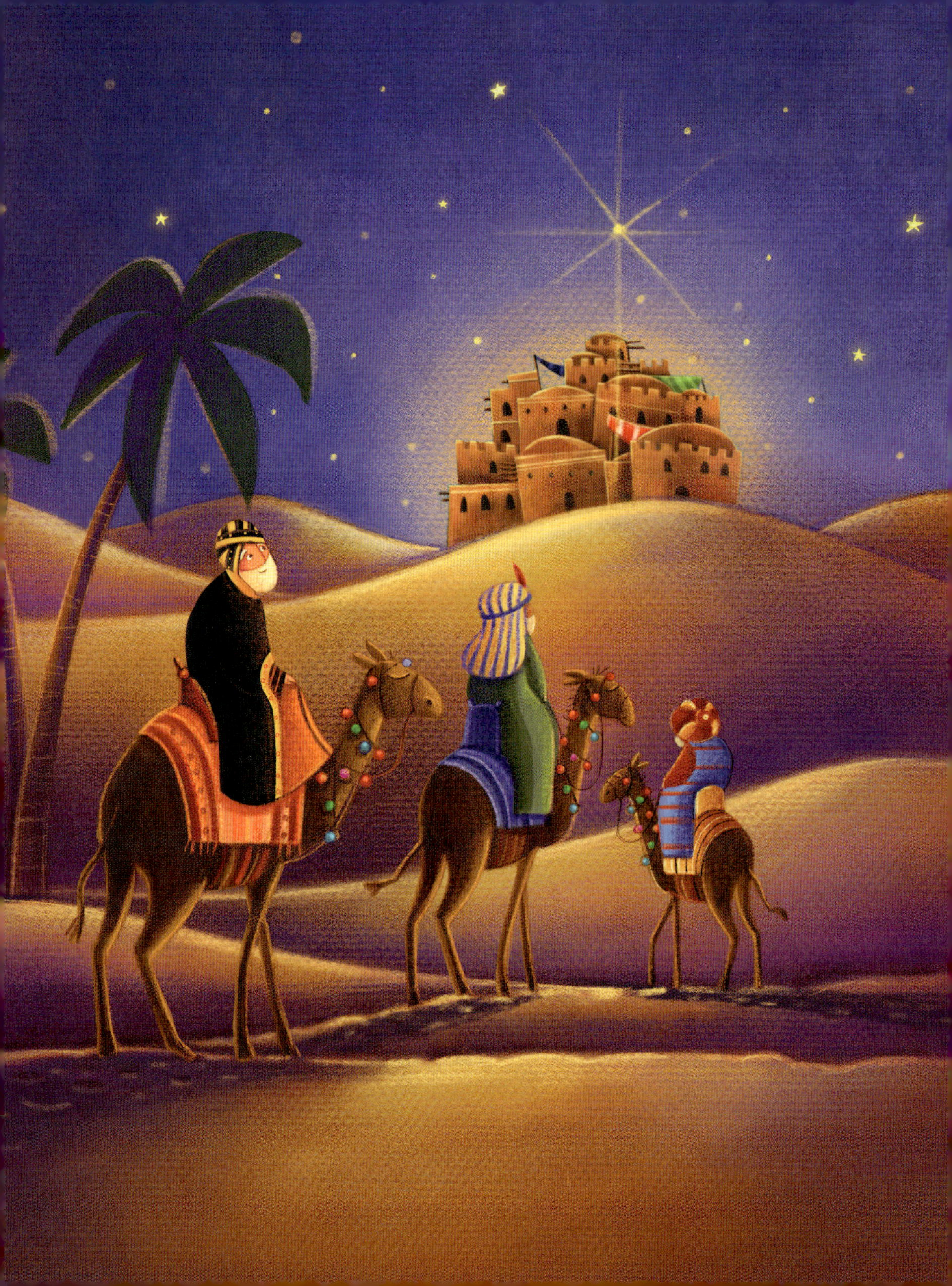

Jesus was worth it, no matter how far!

They loaded their gifts up and rode toward His star.

And when they found Jesus, they worshiped and praised,

Then headed back home again, glad and amazed!

What else? The Bible doesn't say if the wise men rode camels or horses. Both animals are fast, strong, and smart. No matter how they got there, the wise men were overjoyed to worship Jesus.

Like wise people long ago,
We're on an adventure with God.

LET'S GO!

John the Baptist Prepares the Way for Jesus

From Mark 1:1-8

John preached to the people, "God's Kingdom is near. Make the paths straight and make all the ways clear!"

Was John telling people a road should be made,

With bulldozers roaring to smooth out the grade?

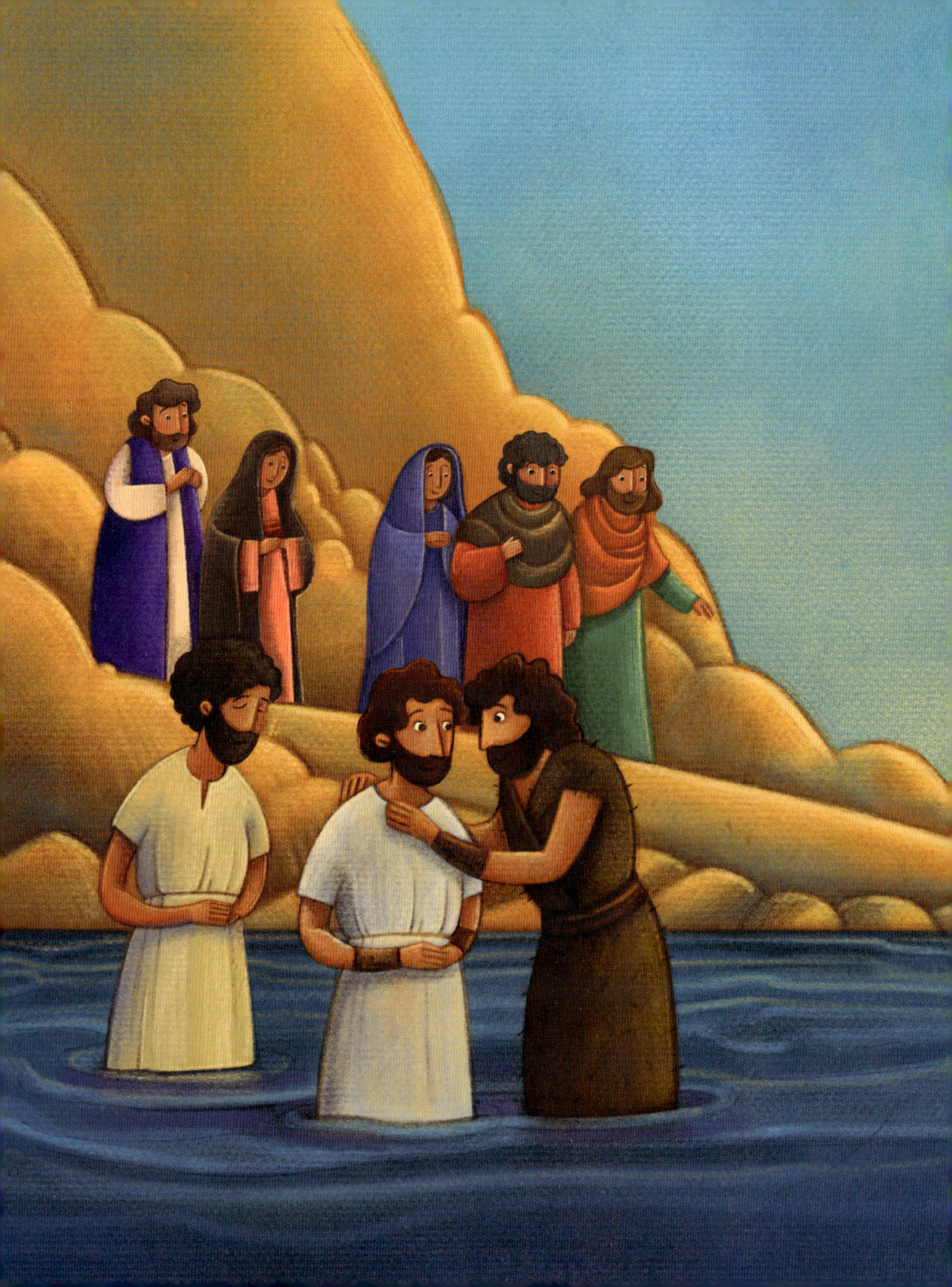

John meant each person should ready their heart,

Turn from their own ways and let God's work start.

He baptized all those who were choosing God's way,

Preparing their hearts for what Jesus would say.

What else? Jesus also came to John to be baptized, and when He came out of the water, "a voice from the heavens said, 'This is My beloved Son, with whom I am well pleased'" (Matthew 3:17).

God's truth can cause our hearts to glow.

We're on an adventure with God.

LET'S GO!

Jesus Teaches the People

From Matthew 4:18-25 and 10:2-4

Jesus grew up, and He did what was right.

He spoke words of life. He showed love day and night.

To help Him teach *more* people God's truth and grace,

Did school buses bring them to one meeting place?

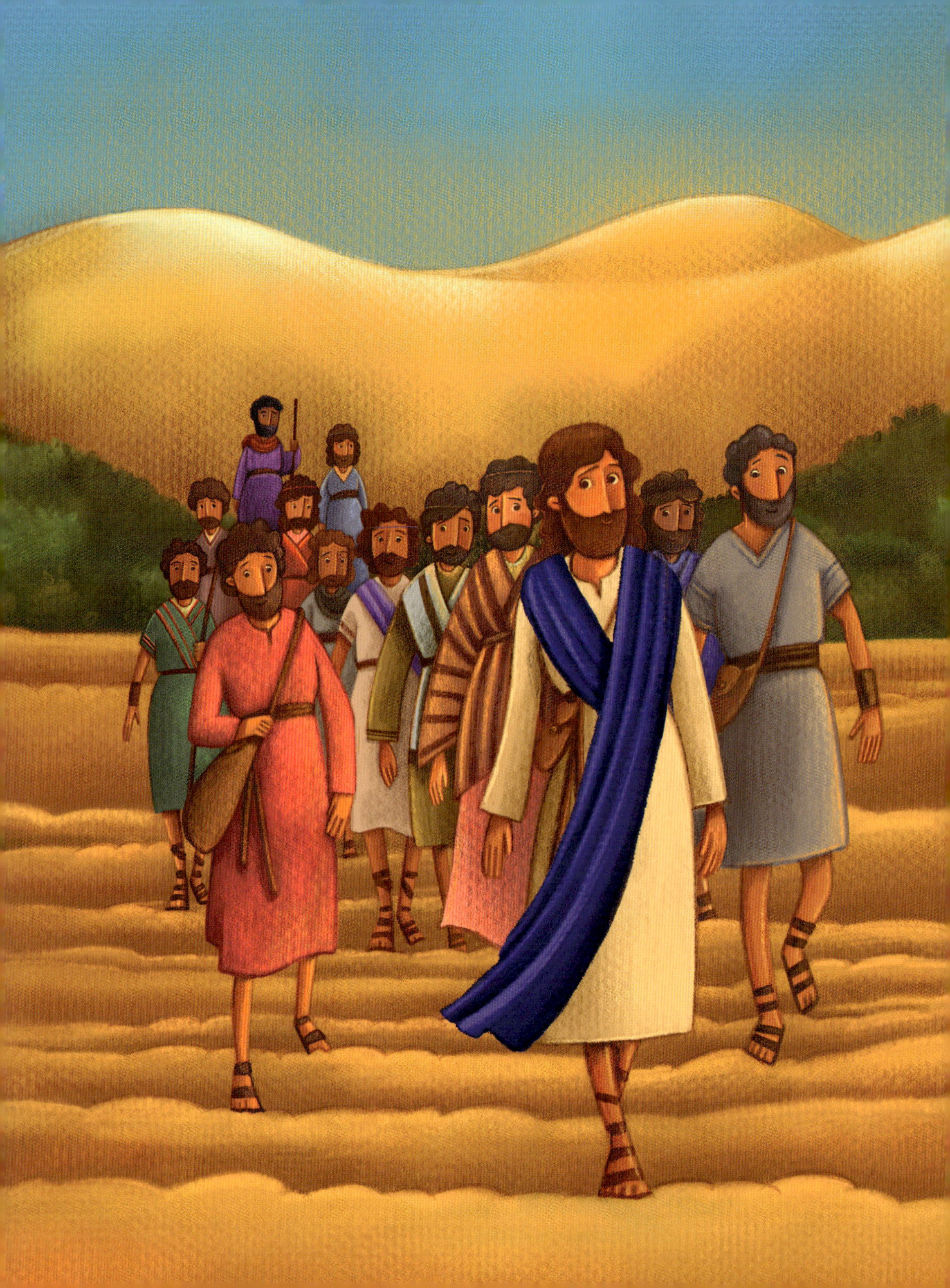

No, He went to *them* to make God's great love known.

Jesus walked far with no home of His own.

He called twelve disciples to serve with Him, too,

And witness the wonderful things He would do.

What else? Jesus taught on mountainsides, from boats, in the temple, by a well, in people's homes, on the shore, near a fig tree, and at many other places.

Back and forth,
to and fro,
We're on an adventure with God.

LET'S GO!

Four Friends Bring a Man to Jesus

From Mark 2:1-12

A man needed healing. His friends had a plan:

"Let's get him to Jesus as fast as we can!"

What could they do since the crowd was so thick?

A small helicopter just might do the trick!

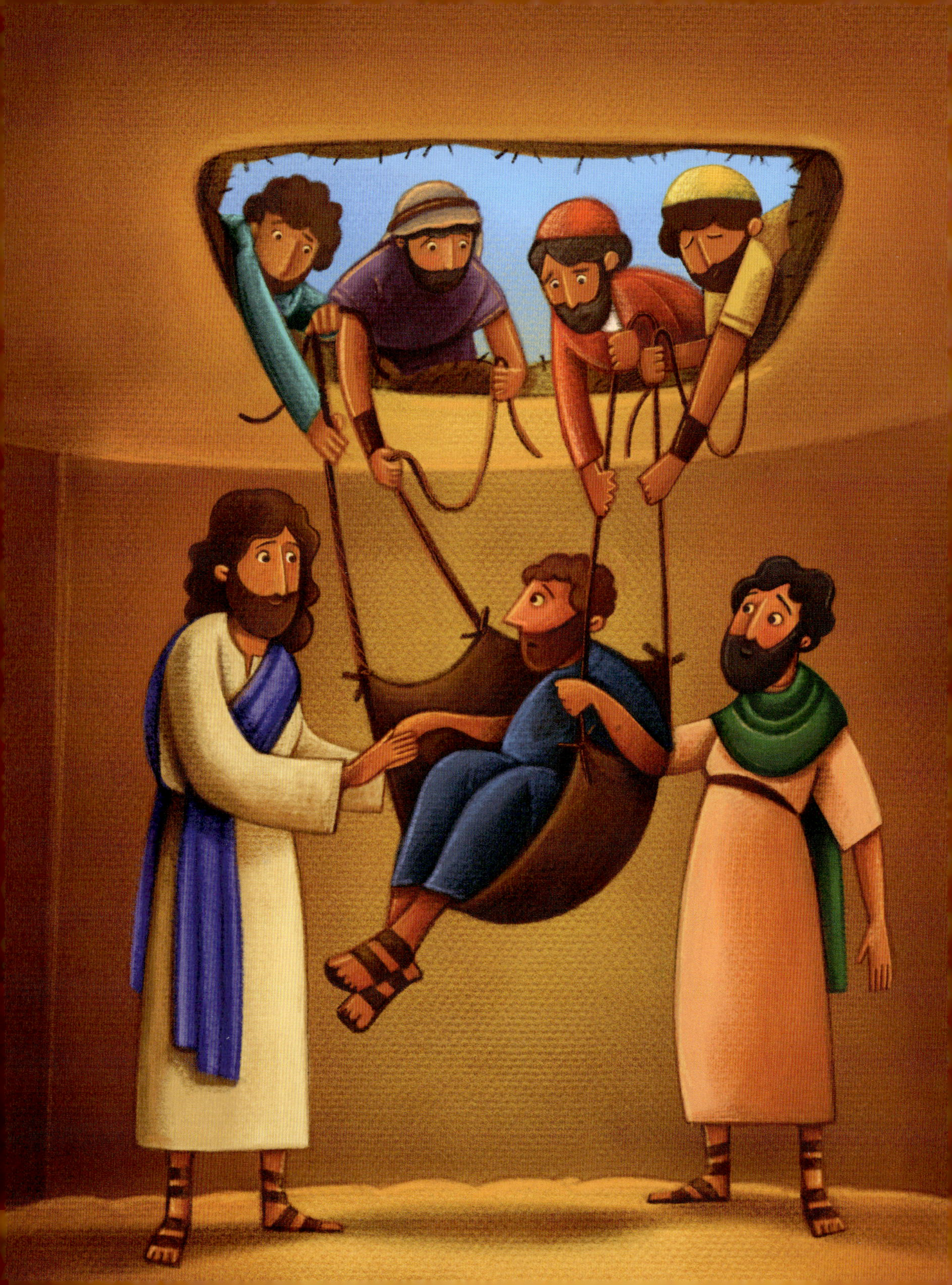

They climbed up, they dug through, they worked with such love.

They lowered their friend from the roof up above.

Seeing their faith and the care they had shown,

The Lord healed the man, and he walked on his own.

What else? Roofs in Jesus' day were made by layering log beams with branches and straw, then covering those with clay.

Even when it's tough and slow,
We're on an adventure with God.

LET'S GO!

A Boy Needs Healing

From John 4:43-53

A boy in Capernaum was desperately sick.

He needed some help, and he needed it quick!

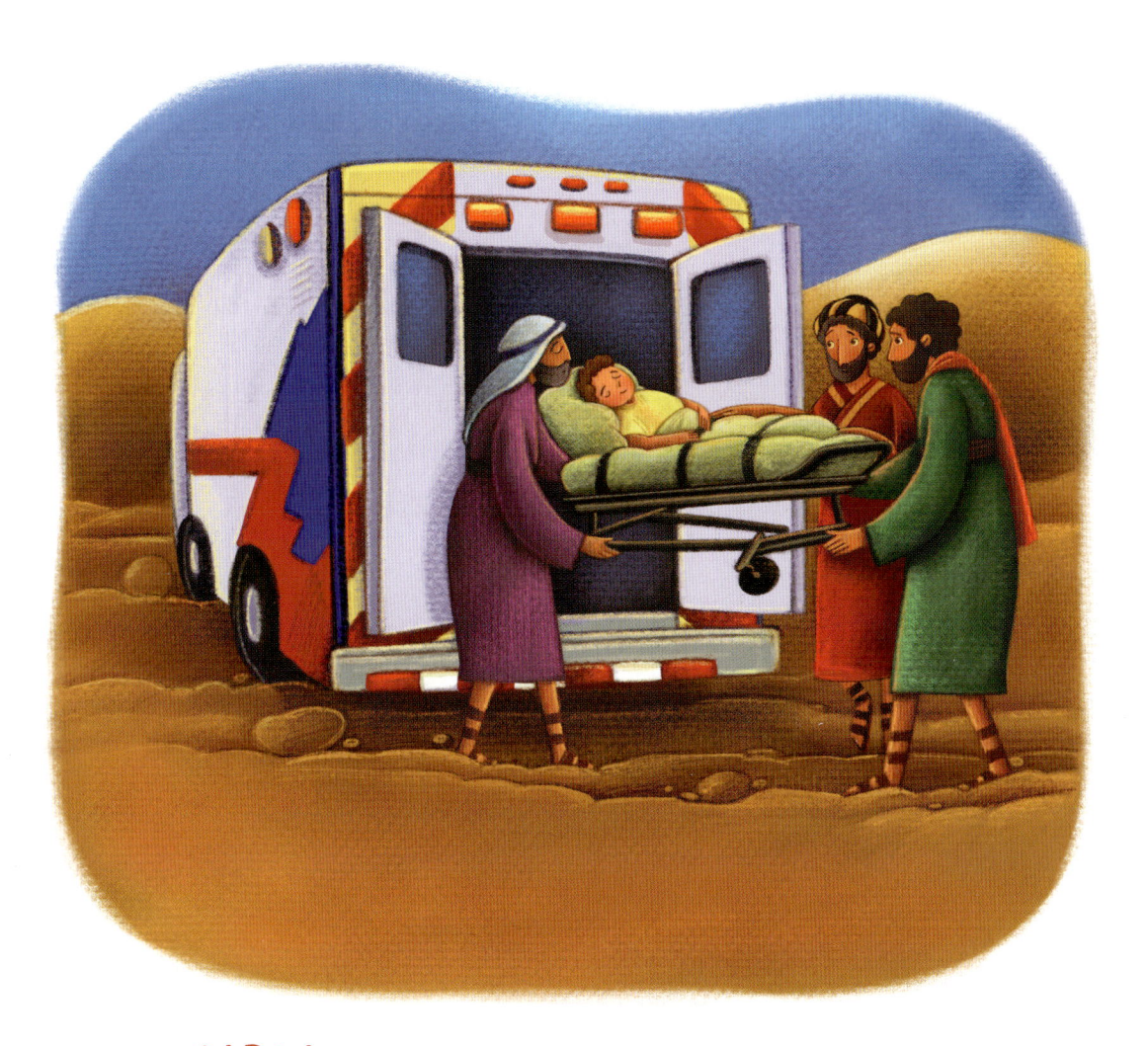

Did Dad call an ambulance? Did Sirens blare?

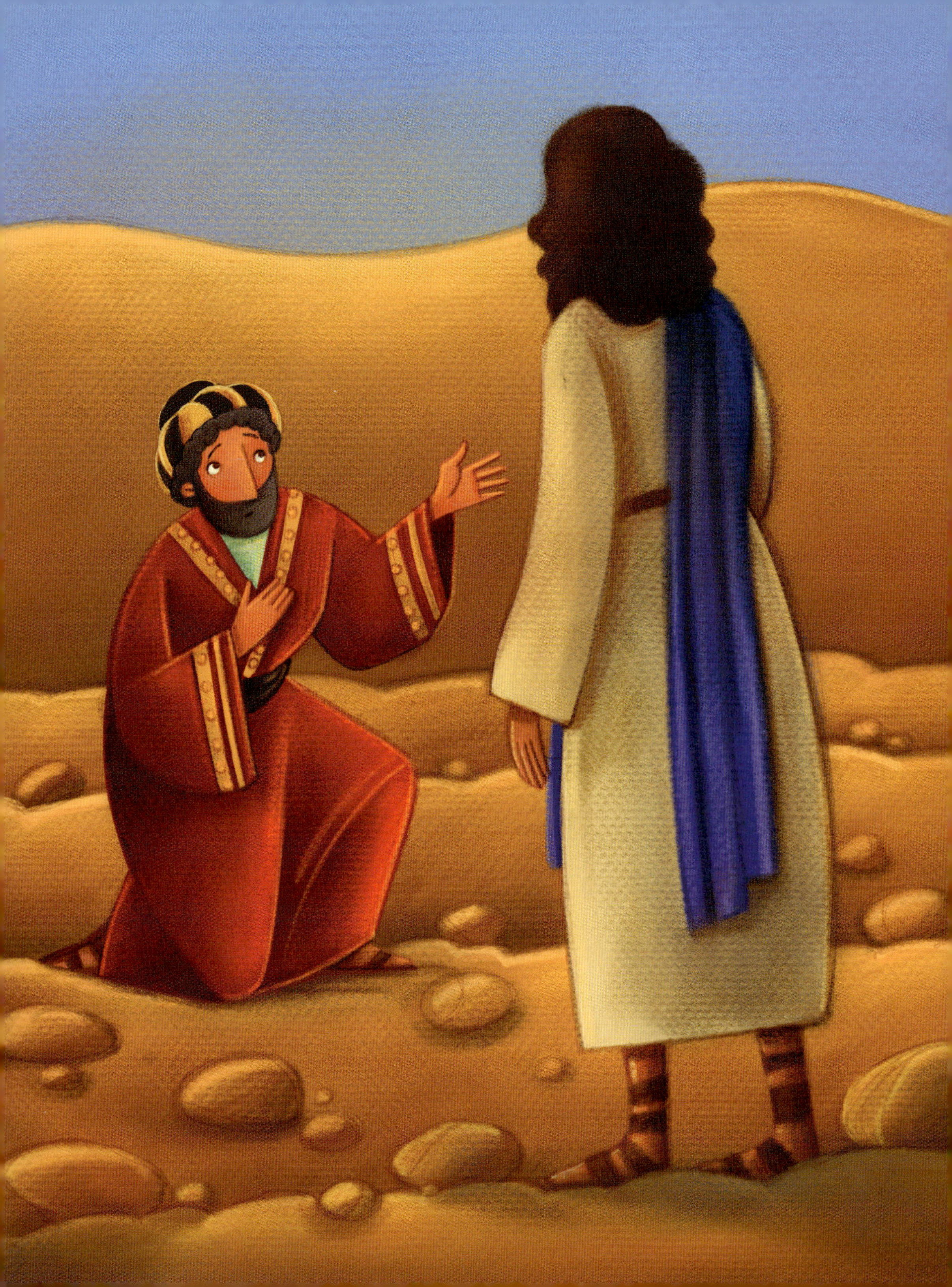

No, Dad went to Jesus, a long way from there.

"Lord, come heal my son," the man started to plead.

Jesus said, "Go see! I've answered your need."

The young boy was healed. He got well right away!

Then all in that house believed Jesus that day.

What else? Jesus healed people who could not see, people who could not walk, people who were very sick—so many people! Jesus also helped people believe God and trust God's love for them, the best healing of all.

God cares for us more than we know.

We're on an adventure with God.

LET'S GO!

Jesus, the Disciples, and the Storm

From Luke 8:22-25

One nice day Jesus said, "Let's cross the lake."

Then He fell asleep while His friends stayed awake.

A fierce storm blew in, and the waves got so rough.

Did they call a rescue boat, speedy and tough?

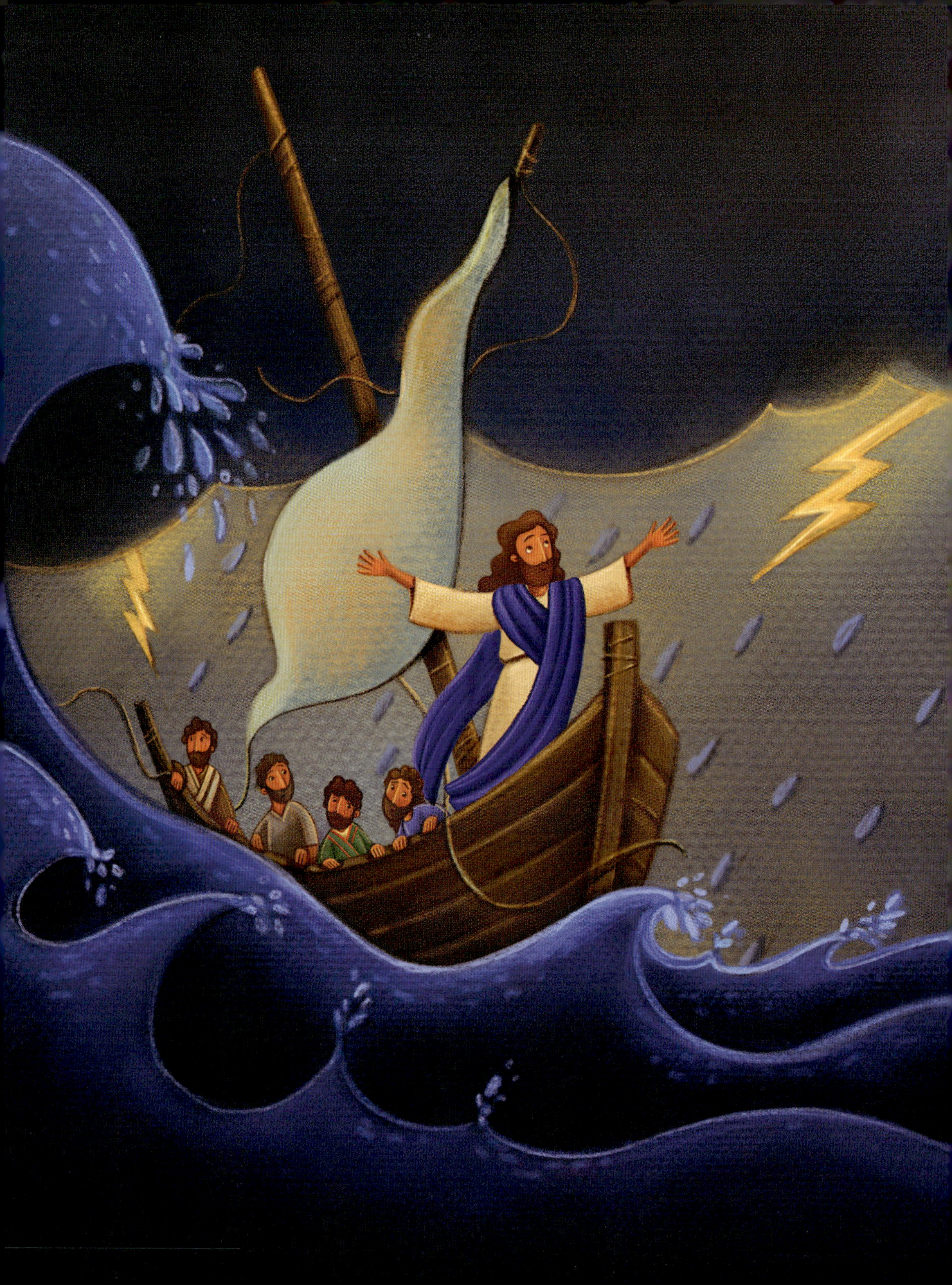

The men shouted, "Help, Lord! We're going to drown!"

The Lord told the winds and the waves to calm down!

They watched the waves stop with their very own eyes.

The storm obeyed Jesus—to their great surprise!

What else? The low walls of fishing boats in that day were great for hauling in a catch of fish but made sailing through storms more difficult.

Trust in God though storms may blow.

We're on an adventure with God.

LET'S GO!

Jesus Feeds More Than Five Thousand People

From John 6:1-13

The crowd wanted Jesus to teach and to heal.

They'd come a long way, and they needed a meal.

Jesus was caring, so what did He do?

call food trucks with tacos and smoked barbecue?

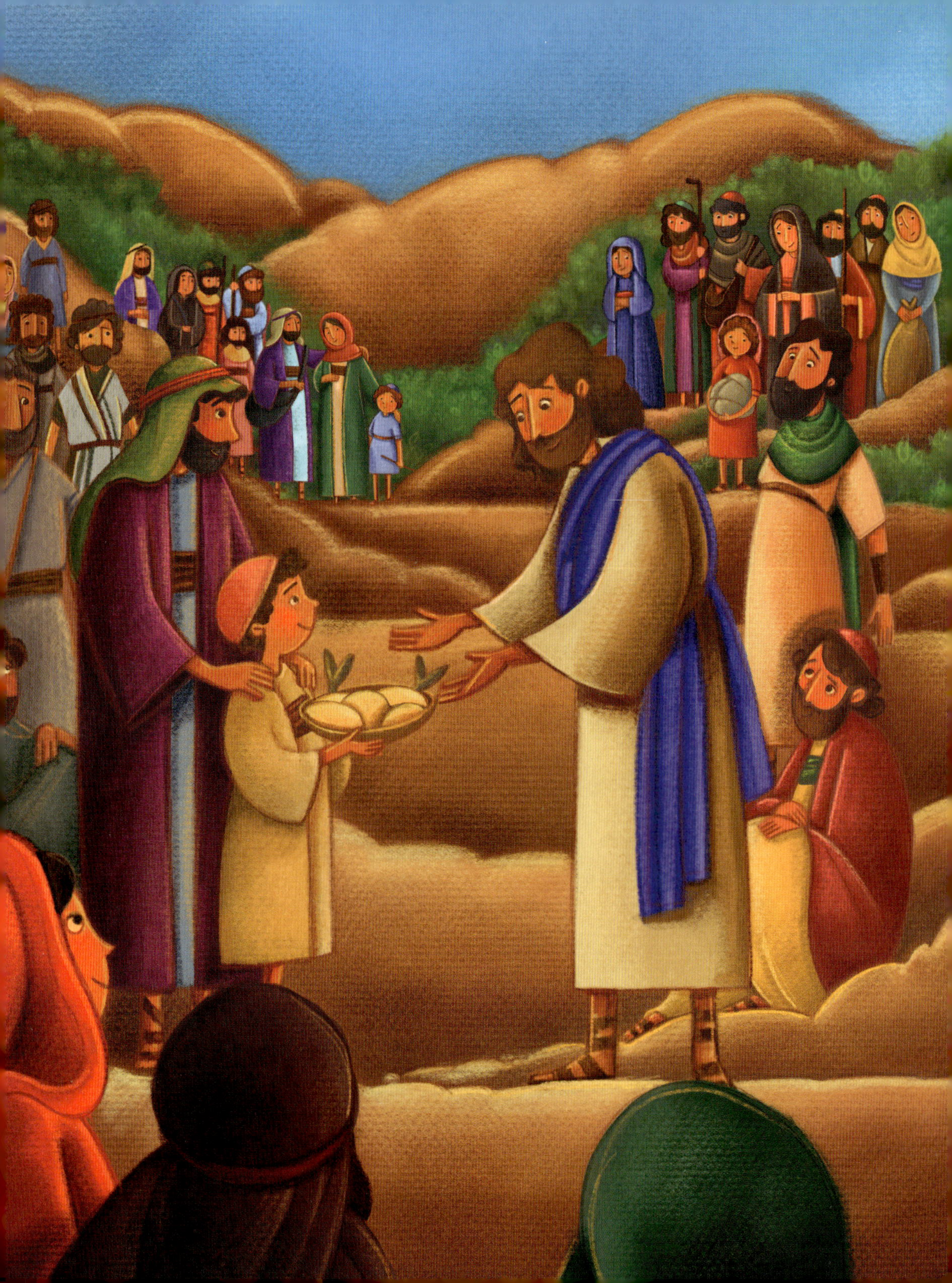

A boy gave his lunch, and although it was small,
Jesus made *more* food—enough food for all.
Disciples passed out yummy fish, tasty bread
'Til thousands of people were happy and fed.

What else? The little boy only had five small loaves of bread and two fish to give to Jesus. But after Jesus blessed it, it was enough to feed more than five thousand people and still have twelve full baskets left over!

God can make
our small gifts grow.
We're on an adventure with God.

LET'S GO!

Jesus Meets the Disciples on the Water

From Matthew 14:22-33

The tired disciples were far from the shore.

Out there in the boat, the wind blew like a roar.

The Lord went to join them, His heart full of care.

Did He ride a Jet Ski to meet them out there?

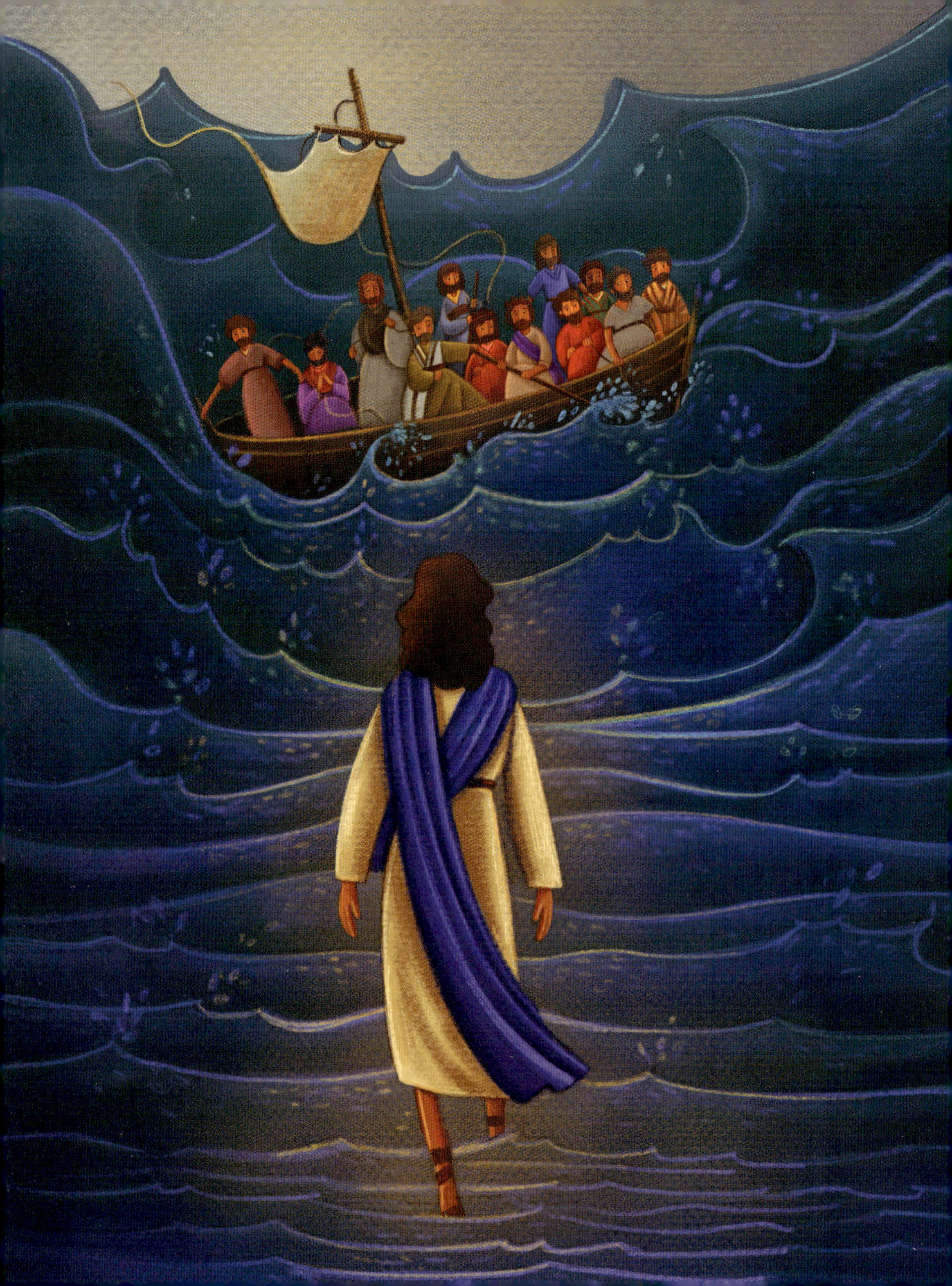

No, Jesus did not need a motor at all.

He walked on the water, and He did not fall!

Then the disciples—astonished and awed—

Praised Him and said, "You're the true Son of God!"

What else? Peter asked Jesus if he could walk on that wild water too, but soon Peter got scared and started sinking! Jesus reached out and caught him, and when they stepped into the boat, the wind got quiet.

Jesus loves us, this we know!

We're on an adventure with God.

LET'S GO!

Jesus and Zacchaeus

From Luke 19:1-10

Zacchaeus, who cheated the people he knew,

Was there in the crowd to see Jesus pass through.

Zacchaeus was short, though, so what did he use?

A tall basket crane with its outstanding views?

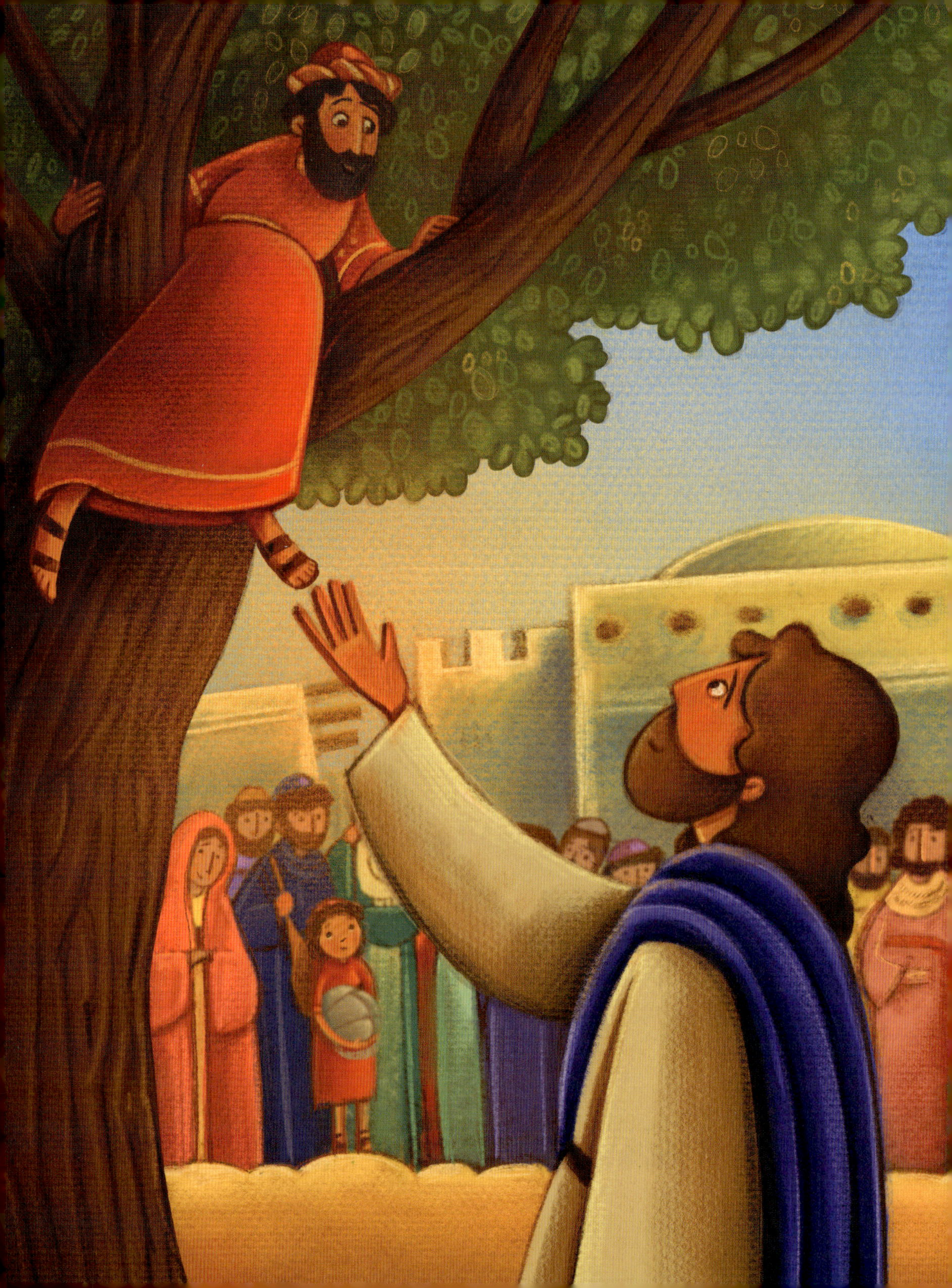

He climbed up a tree, but the Lord called him down.

"I must stay at your house while I am in town."

Zacchaeus said, "Yes!" and then chose to do right.

He gave up his old ways to walk in God's light.

What else? Meeting Jesus changed Zacchaeus, and it showed. He paid people back even more than he took—four times more!

God's grace reaches high and low.

We're on an adventure with God.

LET'S GO!

Jesus and Lazarus

From John 11:1-44

Mary and Martha knew Jesus would care.

Their brother was sick, so they called the Lord there.

Did He go to heal him and make them all smile,

Riding a motorbike mile after mile?

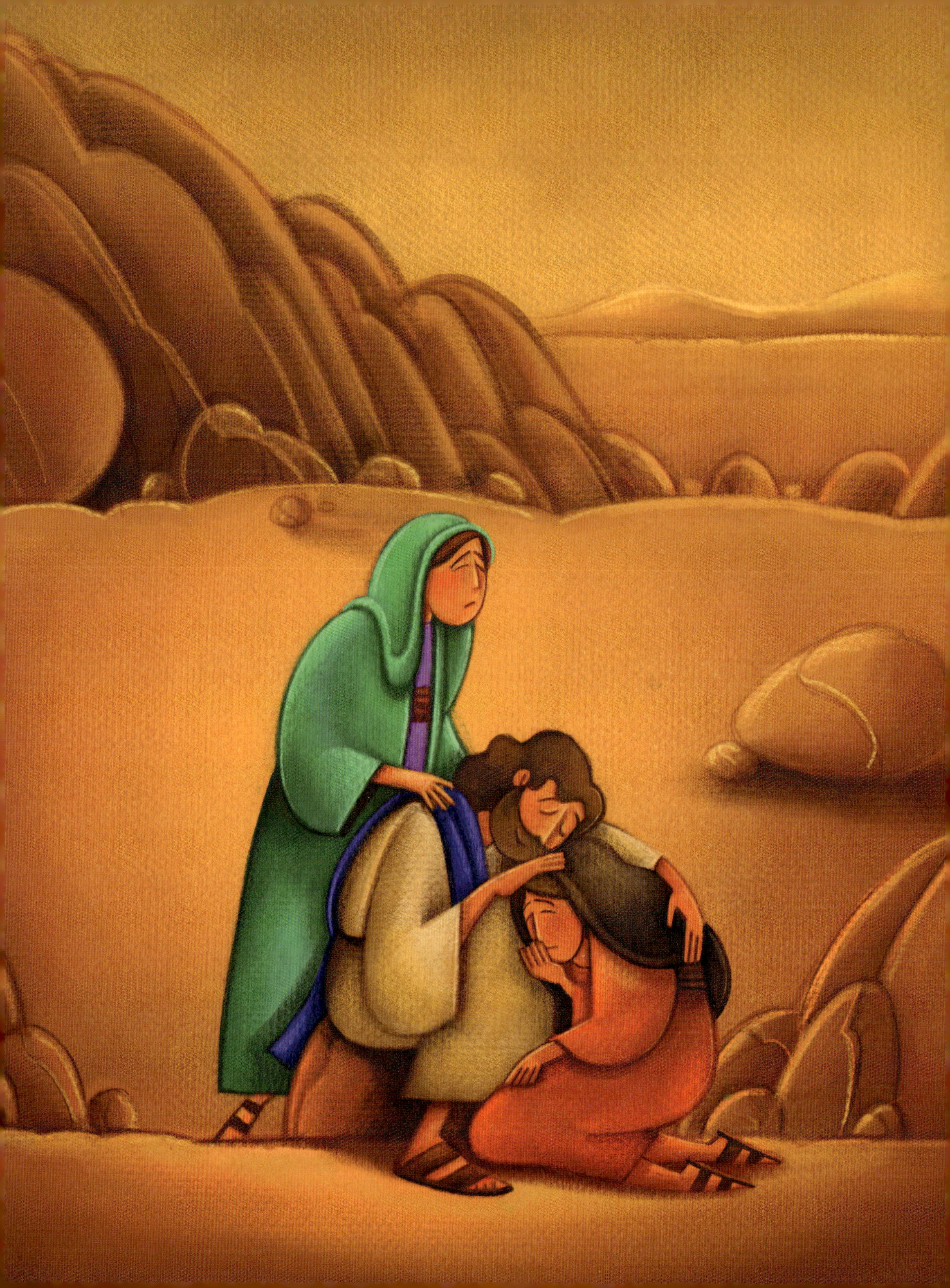

He waited, then walked. His friend Lazarus died.

Though hope filled His heart, the Lord Jesus still cried.

Then Jesus called Lazarus out of the grave!

When things look impossible, God can still save.

What else? The Bible shares three stories of Jesus raising people back to life!

Source of life,
we love You so!

We're on an adventure with God.

LET'S GO!

Jesus Enters Jerusalem

From John 12:12-16

Through crowded streets, loud "Hosannas" did ring!

The crowd was all gathered to welcome a King.

Did Jesus show off His great power and might

And ride a parade float, so flashy and bright?

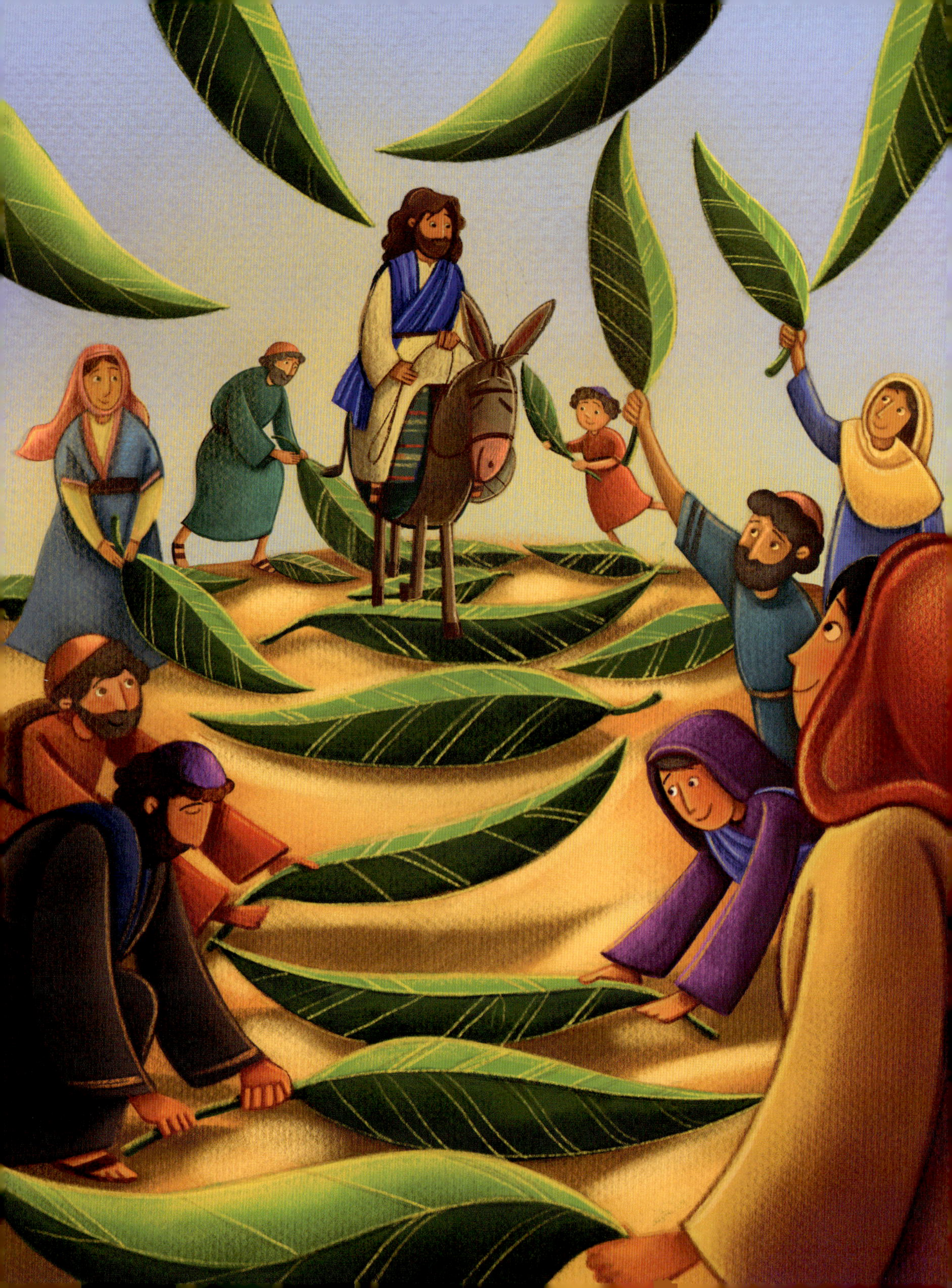

No, Jesus came riding a donkey so small

To show He was peaceful and cared for them all.

Instead of demanding a throne and a sword,

He loved and forgave to show He is the Lord.

What else? The Bible says that Israel's future king would ride a donkey and bring peace (Zechariah 9:9-10). Jesus is the King of everything. He came to bring forgiveness and peace to all who follow Him.

Shout hosanna!
Let praise flow!
We're on an adventure with God.

LET'S GO!

Dirty Streets and Dirty Feet

From John 13:3-17

Roads in that day were not hard like cement.

On dusty dirt streets, sandaled feet came and went.

How did they keep all that gunk off their feet?

Could street sweepers make all the roads nice and neat?

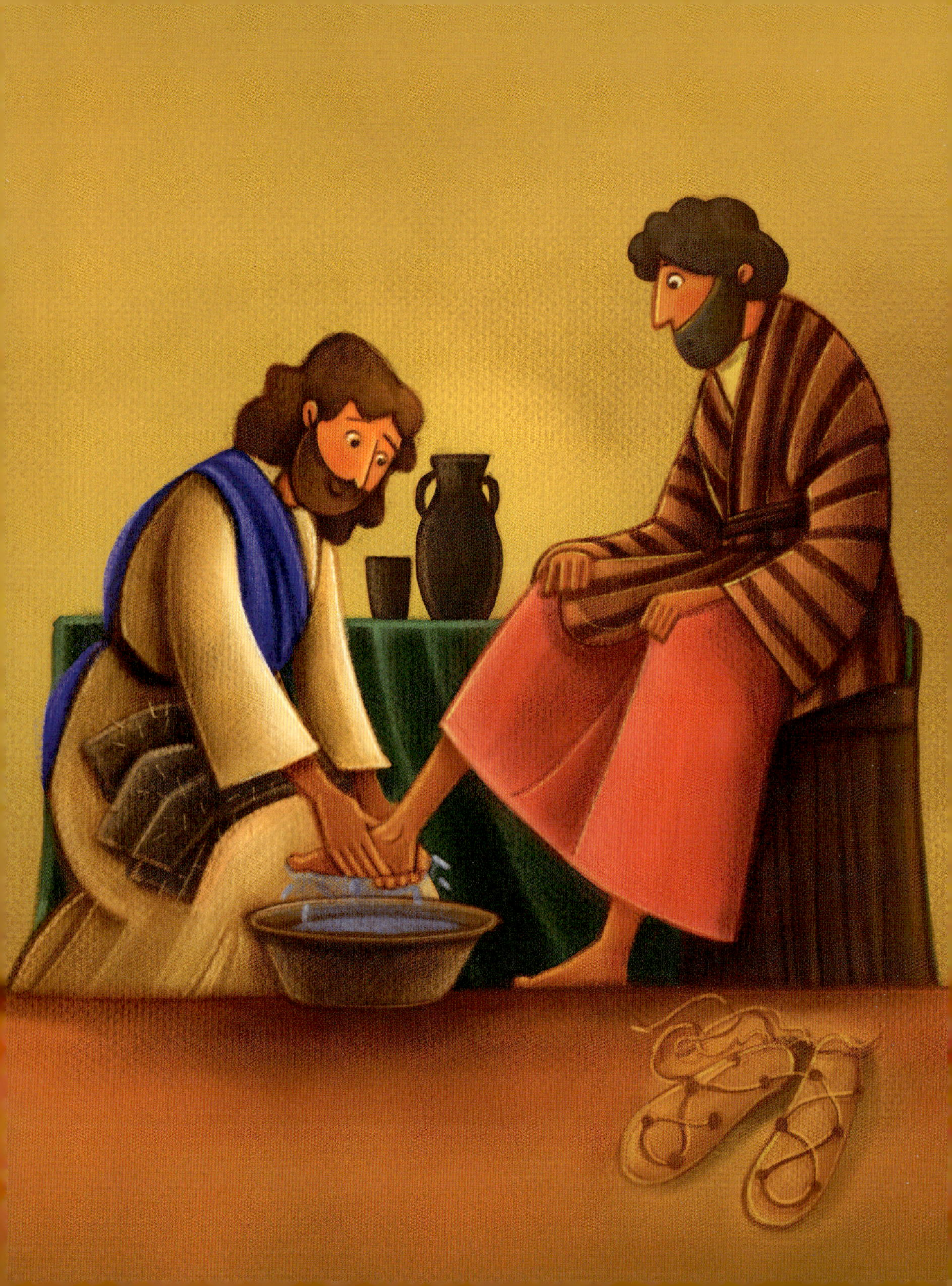

No, dirt streets stay dirty—that's just how it goes.

So they'd scrub their feet, a job nobody chose.

But Jesus knelt down, and He washed their feet clean.

He showed them what *service* and *love* really mean.

What else? After Jesus finished this stinky job, He told His disciples to follow His example and serve with love.

Serve with love
so all will know:

We're on an adventure with God.

LET'S GO!

Jesus Is Arrested

From Luke 22–23

The love Jesus showed and the truth that He shared

Made some men jealous, and their anger did flare!

The leaders made plans to arrest Him at night.

Did search helicopters shine lights bold and bright?

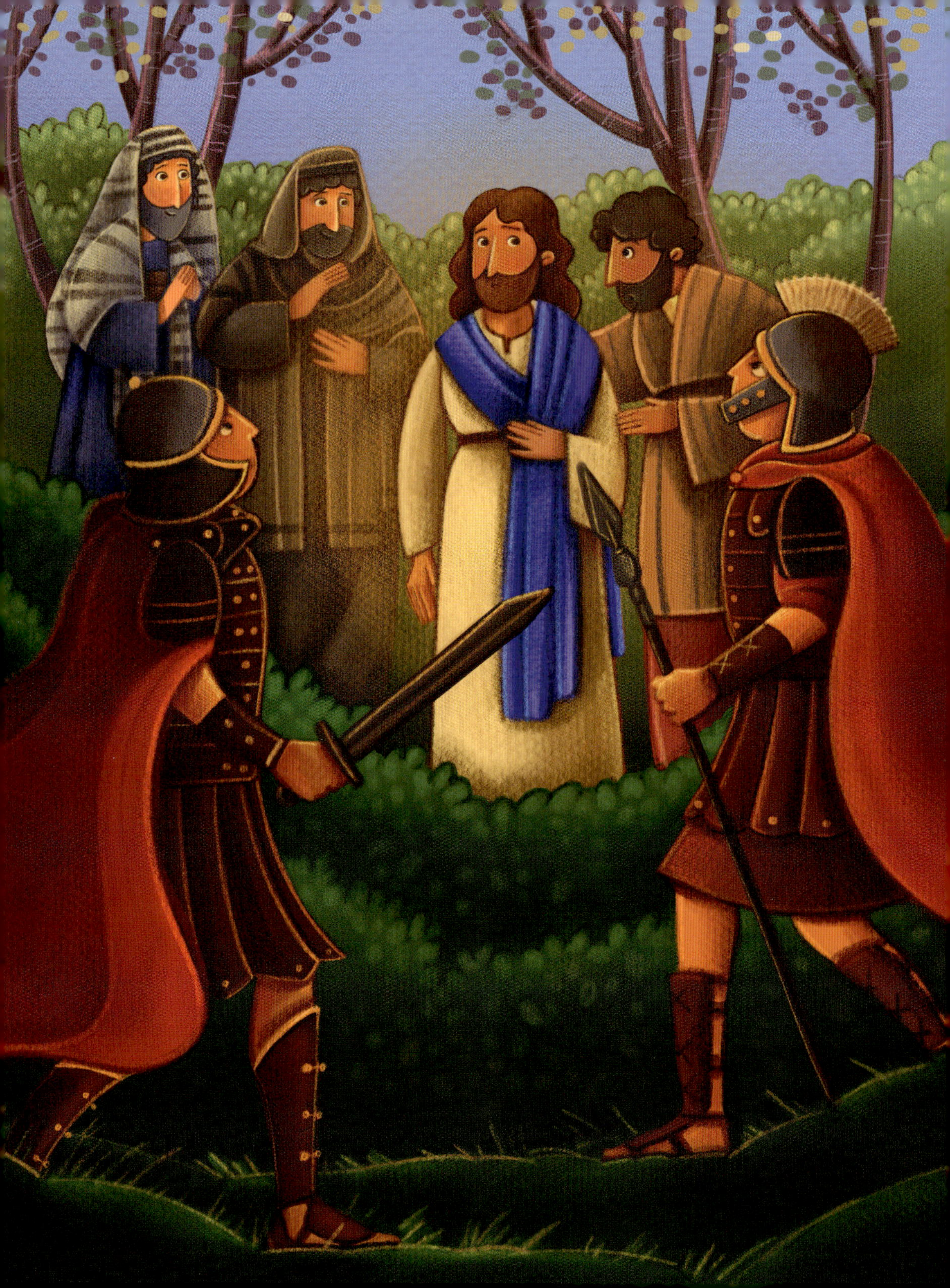

A friend turned against Him and knew where He'd be.

The Lord was arrested and went peacefully.

He died on the cross, our Savior and Friend.

This saddest of sad days was still not the end.

What else? The earth shook and the afternoon sky darkened the day Jesus died. It may have seemed like sin and death had won, but Jesus wasn't finished yet. Keep reading to see the wonderful things that happened next!

In saddest times, hope still can grow.

We're on an adventure with God.

LET'S GO!

Jesus' Resurrection

From Matthew 28:1-8

As friends headed down to the tomb where He lay,

They wondered who'd move the stone out of the way.

How could they open the Lord's sealed-up tomb?

Did they use a crane with its claw and its boom?

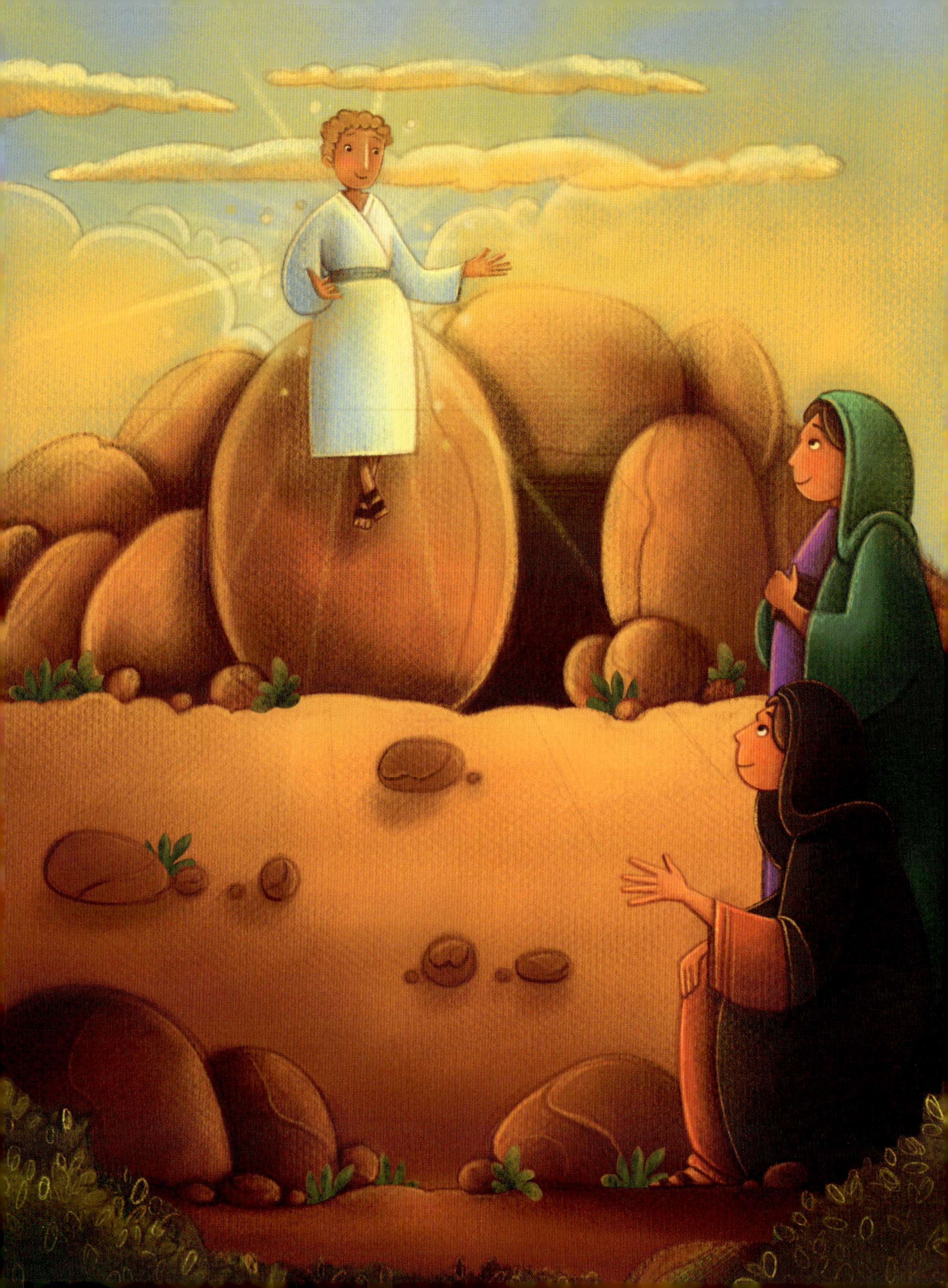

A million times better—a bright angel came,

Rolling the stone away just to proclaim:

"Jesus is risen! Alive! It is true!"

He rose to give new life to me and to you.

What else? The stone covering Jesus' tomb may have weighed as much as a daddy polar bear, a mommy hippo, or a small car. How amazing that it was rolled away to reveal the best miracle of all—Jesus is risen!

Jesus lives!
He loves us so!

We're on an adventure with God.

LET'S GO!

Jesus Ascends into Heaven

From John 14:1-7 and Acts 1:9-11

After He rose, Jesus talked with His friends,

Reminding them His faithful love never ends.

When it was time for the Lord to say bye,

Did a hot-air balloon take Him up high?

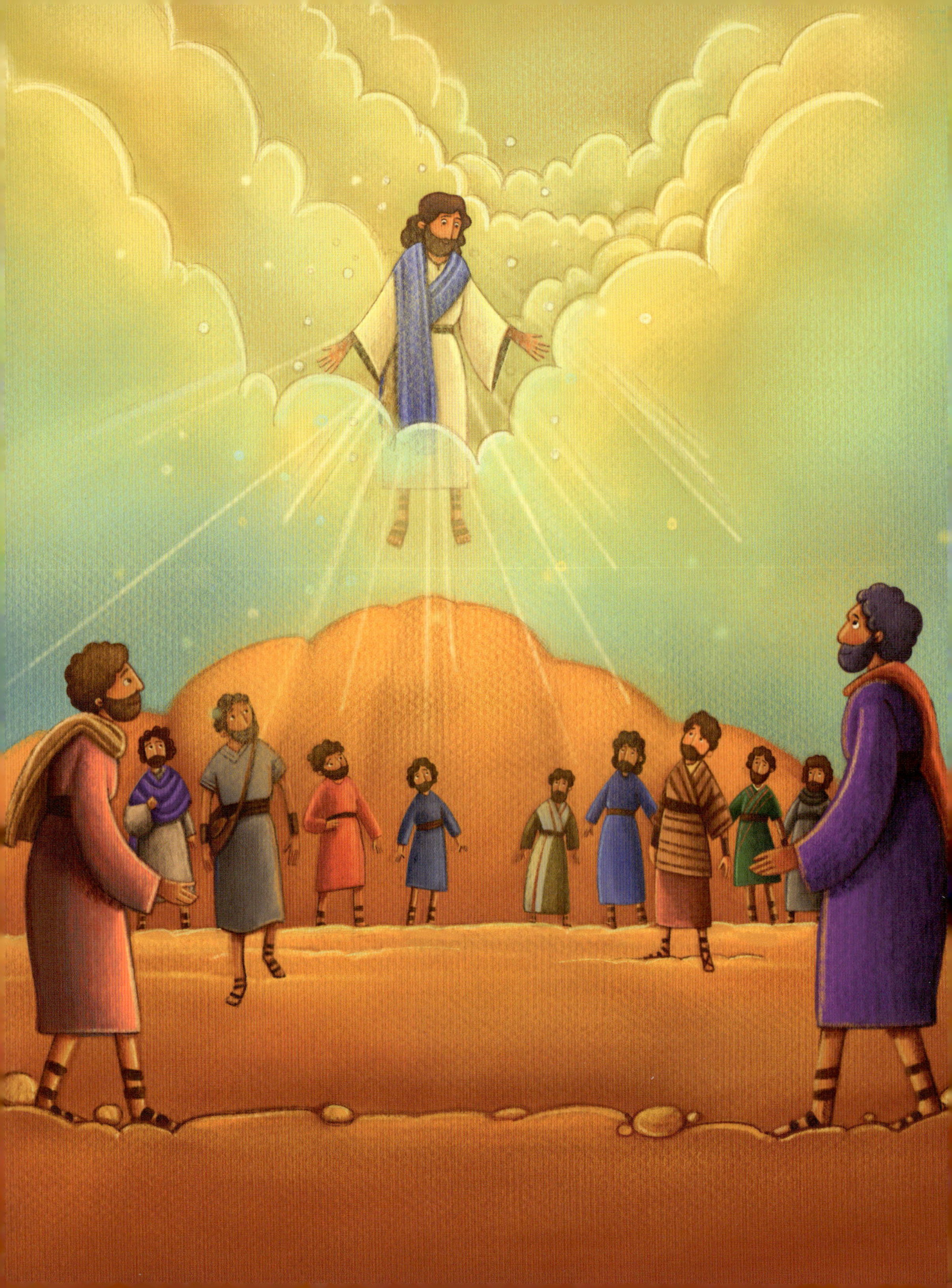

Jesus, God's Son, could go up on His own!
He went up to heaven to God's royal throne.
But that is not all! Jesus went to prepare
A beautiful home for God's children to share.

What else? After Jesus rose from the grave, He appeared to more than five hundred people over forty days before going up to heaven.

We can't see Jesus.
Still we know:
We're on an adventure with God.

LET'S GO!

God Sends the Holy Spirit

From John 14:16-17, 26 and Acts 1:8; 2:1-41

Believers in Jesus all gathered inside—

They needed power, a Helper, a Guide.

A sound like strong wind! Then fiery tongues came!

Did fire truck hoses spray each burning flame?

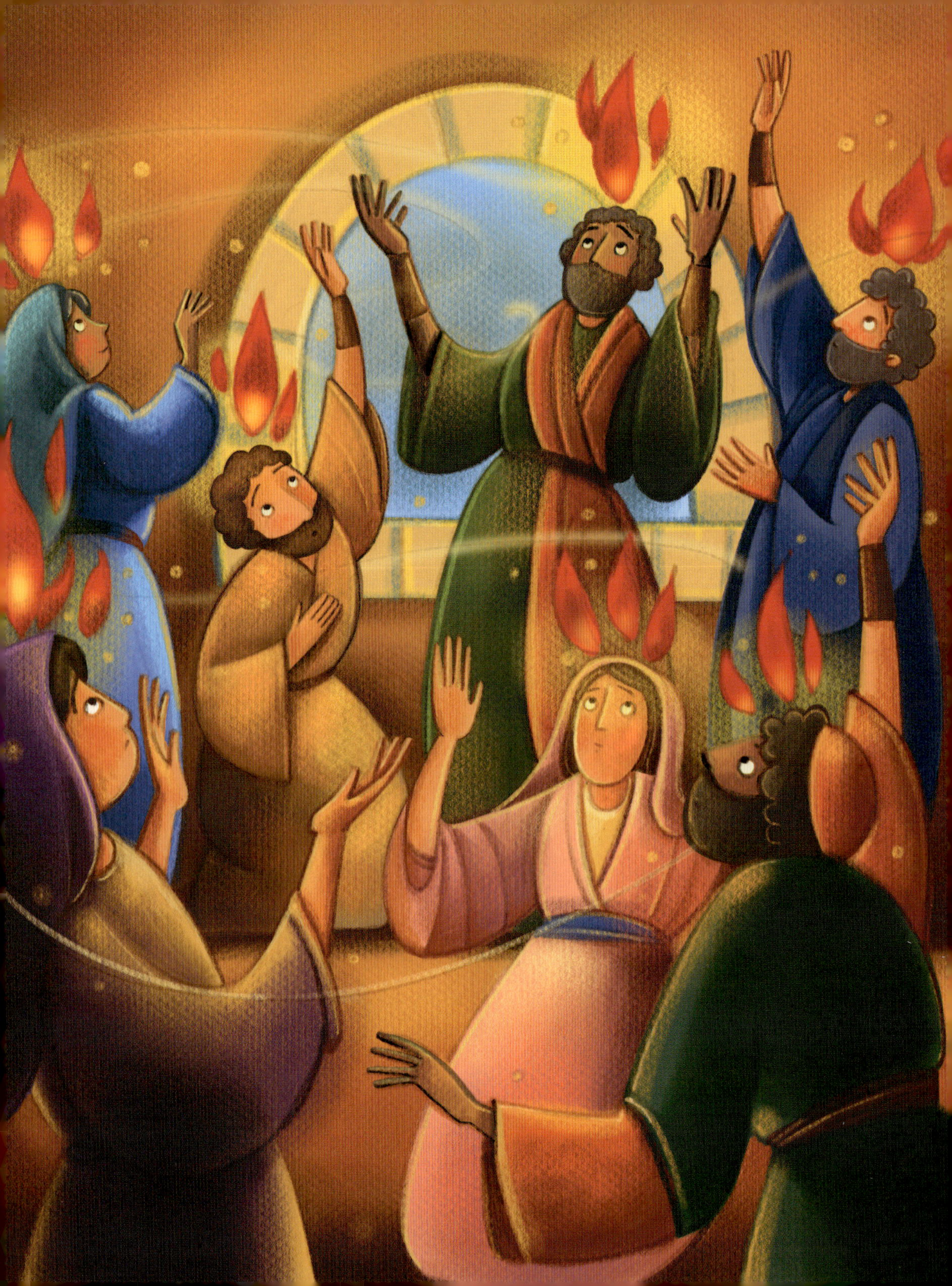

No, this was God's Spirit, as Jesus had said.
The Spirit empowered them—then Good News spread!
In so many languages, God's truth was heard,
And three thousand people believed in God's Word.

What else? People speaking many different languages were visiting Jerusalem for a special feast called Pentecost. The Holy Spirit helped Jesus' followers share the wonderful works of God in each person's language!

We love to see God's Kingdom grow.
We're on an adventure with God.

LET'S GO!

Philip and the Ethiopian Official

From Acts 8:26-40

A man traveled far to the temple to pray.

Then he read God's Word as he went home that day.

But not in a bright-yellow taxi, of course...

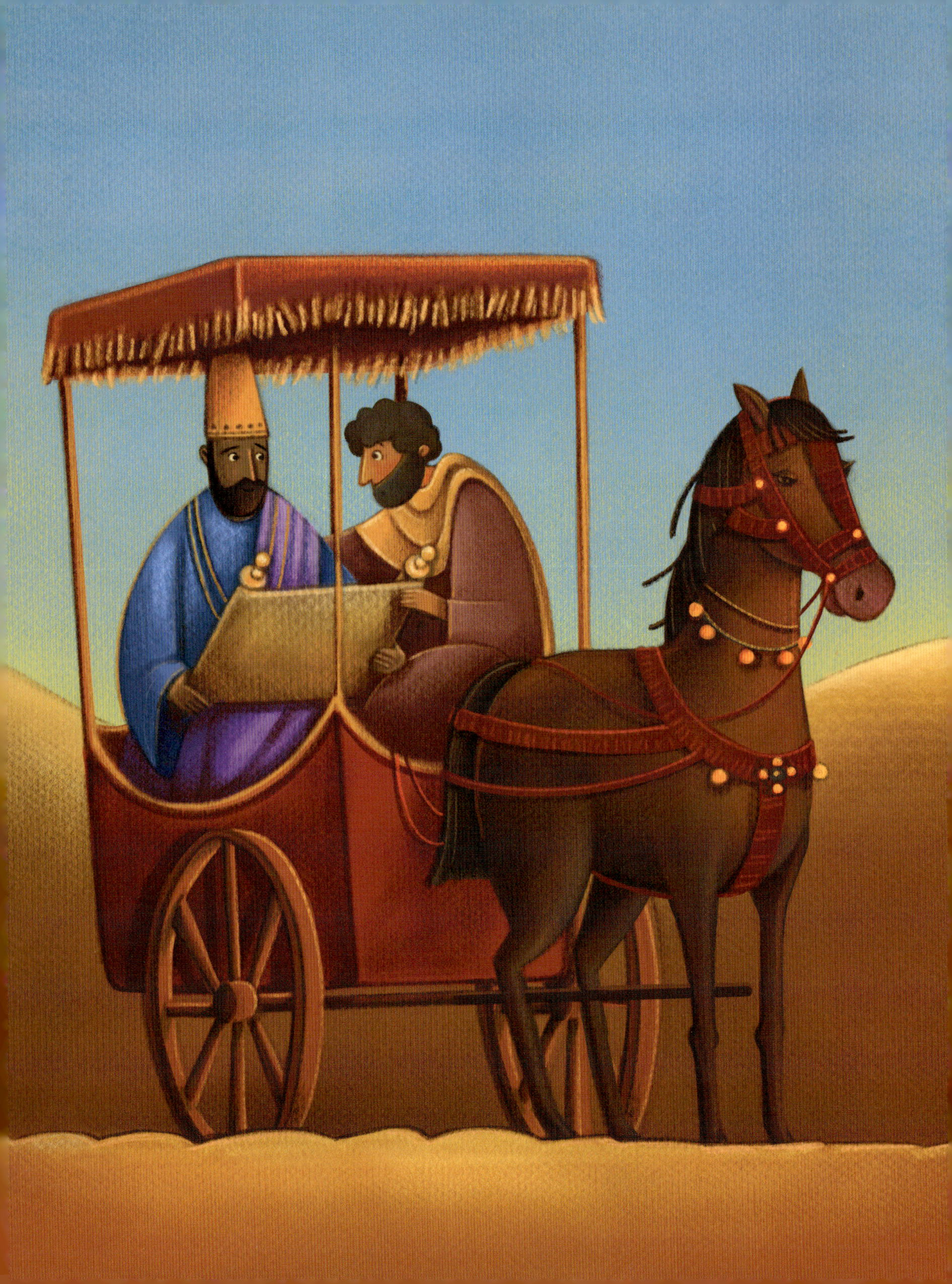

He went in a chariot pulled by a horse!

Then Philip was sent by the Lord to that man

To tell him how Jesus is God's rescue plan.

Excited and glad, the man followed God's way.

He trusted in Jesus that wonderful day.

What else? In Bible times, chariots were the closest things to cars people had. Chariots didn't have motors, but they did have wheels, axles, and a way to steer—the horses' reins.

God's grace is real!
Tell all you know!
We're on an adventure with God.

LET'S GO!

Paul Shares God's Love

From Acts 20:13-24

Paul was so happy—new life had begun!

He had to tell others what Jesus had done.

To share the Good News, he crossed deserts and seas,

But there were no planes to fly high on the breeze.

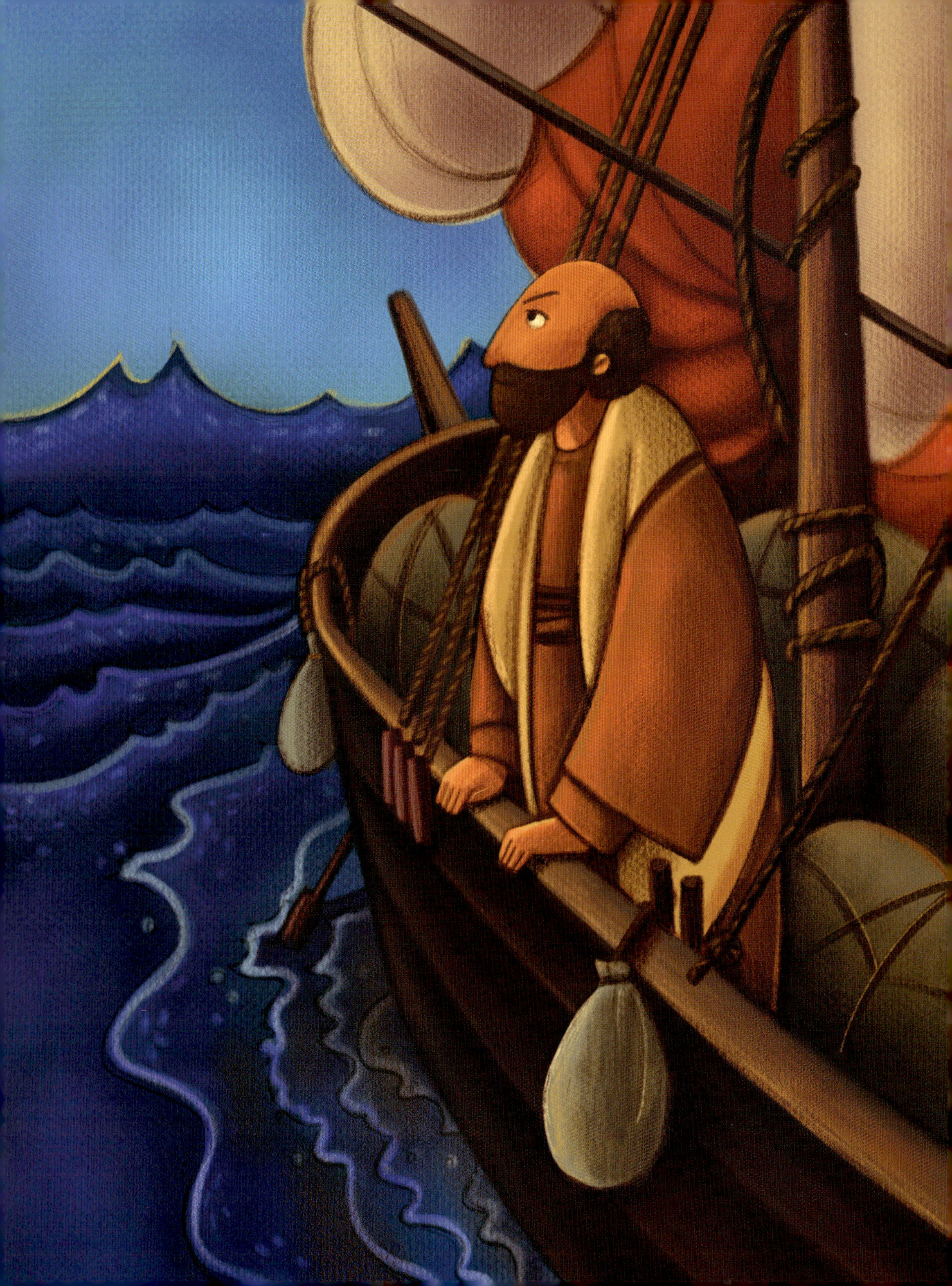

So when it was time to cross water and wave,

Paul got on a ship, sailed the seas, and was brave.

With joy, he told people how much Jesus cares,

How Jesus forgives us and answers our prayers.

What else? Some of Paul's journeys may have been aboard merchant ships with hundreds of other people. Merchant ships carried things people wanted to buy or sell like grain, olive oil, and building materials.

Skies above
or seas below,
We're on an adventure with God.

LET'S GO!

Jesus is Lord! He will come back someday.

He'll make all things new and wipe all tears away.

He'll fill up our hearts with a joy that won't end.

Forever we'll be with our King and our Friend.

God gave us the Bible. It's still true today.

It opens our hearts, and it shows us the way.

Back then, they took chariots, and now we have cars,

But much is the same between their world and ours.

We all need the grace and the love Jesus shows

And God's faithful help through the highs and the lows.

So, through all life's changes, remember it's true:

God's love lasts forever, and God cares for you.

Acknowledgments

What a joy it is to see *Let's Go! Bible Adventures* come to life with the support of so many wonderful people! I am particularly grateful for my agent, Annette Bourland, whose initials also stand for "Above and Beyond." Her thoughtful wisdom, heartfelt cheers, and relentless encouragement have been so meaningful on this journey.

The Tyndale team is a fantastic group to work with! Linda Howard's enthusiastic support, compelling vision, and ongoing collaboration have been true gifts. Karen McGraw deeply understood this project from the start, which was so valuable at every stage. I was blessed with an incredible editorial team in Danika Kelly, Ellen Vosburg, Claire Lloyd, and Cheryl Warner, and I felt their love for God and for kids come through as we worked together. Jackie Nuñez is such a talented art director, and I'm so thankful for the way she and her team beautifully shaped all the visual aspects of the book. I also want to thank Jeff Rustemeyer, Kristen Magnesen, Michelle Polsley, Andrea Martin, Wendie Connors, Emily VanderBent, Natalie Wierenga, and the entire Tyndale team for hosting me at their offices and for being so kind and helpful throughout this process.

My talented critique group—Tiera, Katherine, and Carole—always had the hearts of kids in mind as they devoted their time and attention to this project. I also had an amazing group of friends and family who offered insights into the manuscript and joined me to serve young readers and their families through Our Everyday Parables. A huge thank-you goes out to Karis, Karey, Corrie, Rachel, Joanna, Sarah, Andrea, Leslie, and Leanne!

My parents, Mike and Diane have always done everything they can to support me, and this adventure is no exception. I also treasure each prayer and generous gesture from my fabulous in-laws—Paula, Paul, Jeanette (we miss you so), and Don—and all of Josh's and my wonderful siblings.

My utmost thanks goes to Josh for his loving and sacrificial support. And my heart leaps with happiness when I think of our kids, Gavin and Callen, and all the ways they cheer me on.

Happy tears spring to my eyes when I think of all the ways my faithful Lord has journeyed with me. Even beyond the blessing of this work is the tremendous gift of God's great love, and I'm forever grateful.

About the Author

Valerie Ellis loves helping kids and parents connect with God and each other in the everyday moments. She is an author, speaker, and founder of Our Everyday Parables, an online resource with book reviews and ideas for families pursuing faith and compassion. Valerie lives with her husband, Josh, and their two sons in Houston, Texas, where she stays involved with nonprofits, The MomCo, and SCBWI. Find Valerie at valerieellis.com or @iamvalerieellis on Instagram.

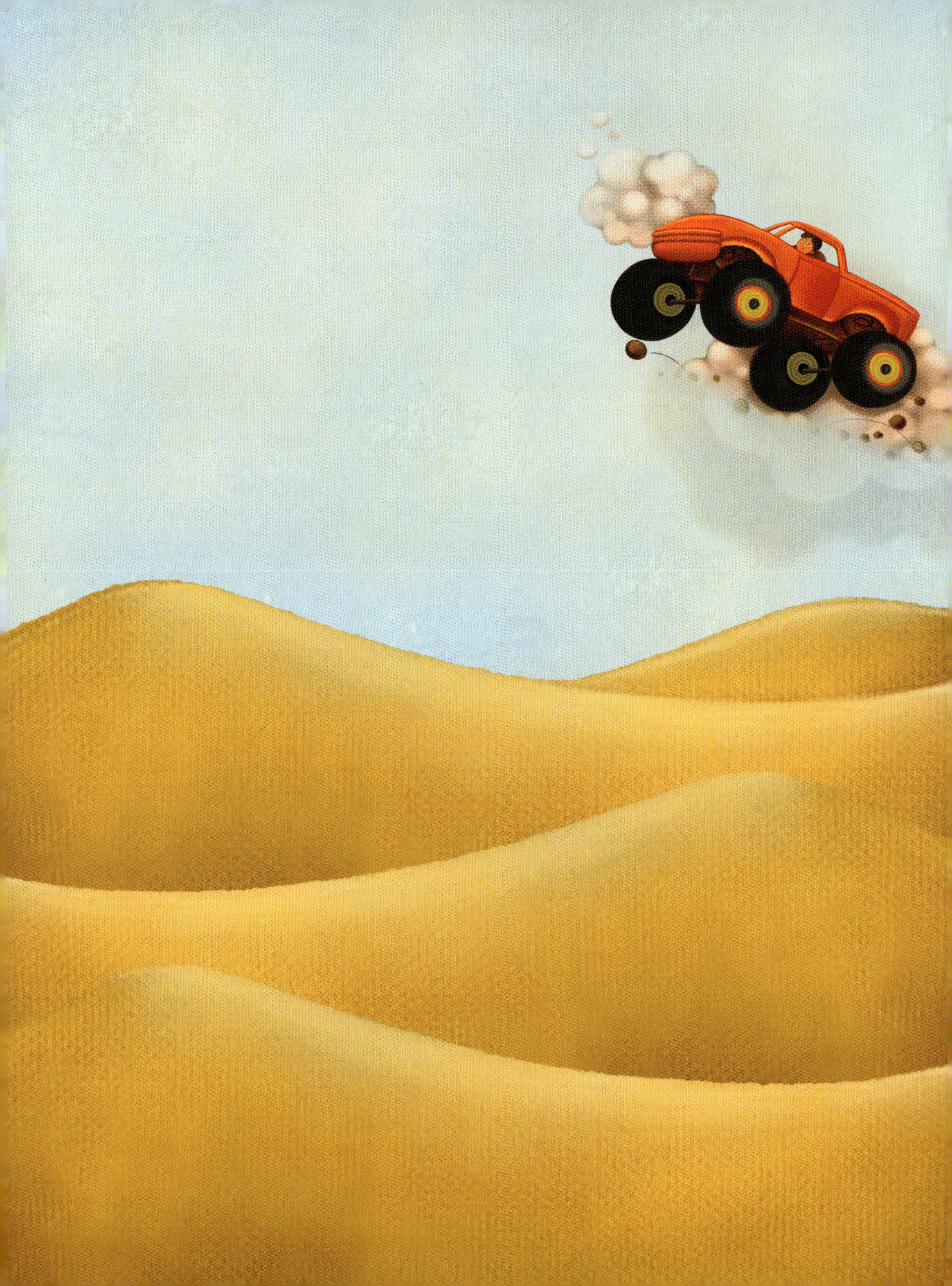